How to Make

FEDERAL MANDATORY

SPECIAL EDUCATION

Work for You

How to Make
FEDERAL MANDATORY
SPECIAL EDUCATION
Work for You

A Handbook for Educators and Consumers

By

ROBERT HAGERTY, Ed.D.

Director of Special Education and Pupil Services
Hazel Park, Michigan Schools

and

THOMAS HOWARD, Ed.D.

Title VI, ESEA, Finance Coordinator
Special Education Services
Michigan Department of Education

With a Foreword by

Harold Wilke, Ph.D.

Faculty Member
Union Theological Seminary
New York, New York
Member, Board of Directors
National Easter Seal Society for
Crippled Children and Adults

CHARLES C THOMAS • PUBLISHER
Springfield • Illinois • U.S.A.

Published and Distributed Throughout the World by

CHARLES C THOMAS ● PUBLISHER

Bannerstone House

301-327 East Lawrence Avenue, Springfield, Illinois, U.S.A.

© *1978, by* CHARLES C THOMAS ● PUBLISHER

ISBN 0-398-03822-8

Library of Congress Catalog Card Number: 78-9643

Printed in the United States of America
R-00-2

Library of Congress Cataloging in Publication Data

Hagerty, Robert.

How to make Federal mandatory special education
work for you.

Includes index.
1. Handicapped children--Education--United
States. 2. Handicapped children--Education--
Law and legislation--United States. I. Howard,
Thomas, 1934-   joint author. II. Title.
LC4031.H33   371.9′0973   78-9643
ISBN 0-398-03822-8

FOREWORD

SEGREGATION has been a fighting word for me for most of my life. I have worked toward integration. It is the inclusive, the whole, the matrix which is ultimately important. The parts, whether of a plan or a program or of society, need to be studied, of course; their place in the total structure must be understood.

This excellent book by Dr. Robert Hagerty and Dr. Thomas Howard, helps us see one group — one section — of this population of ours which requires education, and at the same time sets that section — that special group — within the context of the whole.

The underlying assumption is that there is no wholeness without the inclusion of each part, and most especially this part, the disabled and handicapped.

For the handicapped may well be said to be America's last great minority. They have been ignored, shunted, institutionalized. They have been forced into positions where they are "out of sight" and therefore "out of mind." The educational system, rather than redirecting and changing this situation, perpetuated it by barring handicapped children at the school door.

I was one of those barred at the school door.* I got into school because a one-room country schoolhouse was willing to accept me. Fortunately, there are and have been cracks in the whole system, and I was able to get on for education and/or degrees at the University of Chicago, the Union Theological Seminary, Harvard and other institutions. It was not "Look, Ma, no hands!"; it was rather a serious involvement in education that said a handicapped person could indeed carry his own weight, and in my own case, I like to think, make at least some

---

*A schoolteacher said, "We cannot accept a student who writes with his toes because all the other students will watch him and no longer pay attention to their own lessons."

contribution to the world.

Now we are no longer dependent on the whim of administrators. Congress has passed a bold new law requiring all school districts in the nation to open their doors to handicapped children, in Public Law 94-142, the Education of all Handicapped Children Act.

Thomas Howard and Robert Hagerty are veteran administrators in special education and in this book have filled a void for educators as well as parents, bringing together the best information from field-based professionals as to how to implement this new act. Further, the authors have addressed the hasty and often erroneous interpretations which have surrounded the act.

The legal requirements of the act are here translated into insightful and practical suggestions for local school programming, providing also abundant examples from those who are doing well.

Unique in concept and development, the book is not a theoretical study of the problems of the new law, but rather develops concrete avenues as to how the law can be made to work to benefit handicapped children.

In the first part of the Federal Mandatory Special Education Act, the authors recite some of the history of federal legislation for the handicapped, including the court struggles where rights for the handicapped were won. Here is a sound historical perspective behind the revolutionary new law.

The second part is an invitation to see how this new law can change the school lives of handicapped children. The authors indicate how local education agencies can effectively implement the law, and they call attention to ways of identifying and providing quality programs for the preprimary handicapped.

At the point where government officials, school administrators and parents truly understand the mandatory law and begin working together, successful implementation of the Special Education Act will occur. This argument is supported by the book's discussion of three guidelines of three critical areas for quality education of the handicapped: (1) establishing guidelines for the effective management of the new law by states and local education agencies, (2) developing procedures for successfully working with parents in the implementation of the mandatory law, and (3) establishing sensible guidelines to make mainstreaming work.

Ranging from teacher training to practical ways of making schools barrier-free, Thomas Howard and Robert Hagerty offer proven, success-oriented techniques already being used in many schools across the country to demonstrate that this old new law can really be effective.

New York   Harold H. Wilke

PREFACE

SINCE the Education for All Handicapped Act became law, it has been discussed and debated by virtually every segment of the education community. These discussions have centered around many unanswered questions related to the implementation of the Act.

The purpose of this book is to look at the many ramifications of the Act and to provide some rational direction to the professional educator and the consumer for translating the Law into reality.

To help the reader understand how the Act came to be, we have traced the history of the struggle for rights for the handicapped, and indicate how most of the present pressures have their roots in the influences of the past.

Our first-hand experiences at both the state and local level in the implementation of Michigan's far-reaching Mandatory Law (P.A. 198) have provided a sound background for a rational analysis of P.L. 94-142.

We have taken issues which have created the greatest national concern and explored each one objectively. We analyze the requirements of P.L. 94-142, what it requires, what it does not require, and what the responsibilities of others are. It has been our experience that most administrators, teachers, and parents sincerely wish to do their best for the handicapped, but they are often confused by the lengthy legal jargon and the frequent misinterpretations of this revolutionary new law.

It is our desire that this book will bring about a closer alignment of all educators and parents, a goal that is desirable so that all children can receive an appropriate education.

We have lived through the implementation of nearly every requirement of P.L. 94-142. As administrators of special education at the state and local levels, we have seen the dreams of

Michigan's P.A. 198 go from promise to reality.

We hope that this book will challenge both practitioners and consumers to aspire to creative leadership and to expand their horizons so that the free and appropriate education called for in the Education for All Handicapped Act will become a reality.

Advocates and detractors of the law will attempt to use emotional rhetoric to sway those responsible for the implemenation of the Act. We urge you to thoroughly read each chapter of the book. Knowledge of this new educational policy as outlined in the pages to follow will be necessary to design and implement good programs for the handicapped.

ACKNOWLEDGMENTS

THE many state departments of education who responded so generously to requests for mandatory special education management data are sincerely thanked. In particular the state departments of Indiana, Michigan, Ohio, Florida, Pennsylvania, Maryland, and Arizona were helpful.

Special recognition is given to David Savage and the assistance he rendered through the National School Public Relations Association.

Grateful acknowledgement is given to the Council for Exceptional Children whose data research bank helped make this project much easier.

Reliable assistance was also provided by Frank Wawzraszek, Professor of Special Education, Eastern Michigan University and Charles Mange, Chairman Department of Special Education, Michigan State University.

R.H.
T.H.

INTRODUCTION

O N November 29, 1975, President Ford signed P.L. 94-142, a federal law guaranteeing a free and appropriate education to all handicapped children. Approved in the Senate by an 83 to 10 vote on June 18, 1975, and a subsequent 375 to 44 affirmation in the House of Representatives on July 29, Congress ushered in a new public education policy.

Leading up to the passage of the Law, Congress learned the following in legislative hearings:

- Over 1.75 million children with handicaps in the United States were being excluded entirely from receiving a public education solely on the basis of their handicap.
- Over half of the estimated 8 million handicapped children in this country were not receiving the appropriate educational services they needed and/or were entitled to.
- Many other children with handicaps were still being placed in inappropriate educational settings because their handicaps were undetected or because of a violation of their civil rights.

In many ways Congress saw the handicapped as America's last great minority, and they saw the need for a national effort to remedy the discriminatory practices which were evident through testimony. Congress decided this effort should take the form of a "Bill of Rights for the Handicapped."

As a result of P.L. 94-142, groups of teachers, administrators, and parents are in varying states of confusion regarding what to do, when and how to do it. Interpretations of the Act are as varied as the number of special educators and administrators who endeavor to make some meaning out of it. Clever advocacy groups, boards of education, and administrators attempt to fit the act to their parochial biases.

The appropriate implementation of P.L. 94-142 will come about as a result of some basic training and understandings of the Act.

CONTENTS

How to Make

FEDERAL MANDATORY

SPECIAL EDUCATION

Work for You

Chapter 1

THE ROLE OF FEDERAL LEGISLATION IN PROVIDING EDUCATION FOR THE HANDICAPPED

THE opening day of school in September 1978 marks the end of a quiet revolution to achieve public policy affirming the right to an education for children with handicaps. On that date, P.L. 94-142, the Education for All Handicapped Children Act of 1975 becomes fully effective.

Actually, federal support for education of the handicapped goes back a century and more, to 1864 and the establishment in Washington, D.C. of Gallaudet College, serving the deaf; and to 1879 and the creation in Lexington, Kentucky, of the American Printing House for the Blind. Valuable though these actions were, however, they did not signal a Federal commitment to education of the handicapped. In the 1930s, the U.S. Office of Education, by then more than sixty years old, first assigned a member of the staff to monitor the condition and progress of "special education," as education of the handicapped was by then being called. Neither did this action indicate a federal commitment to education of the handicapped.

A significant shift in posture was (quietly) launched in 1954 when the Congress passed legislation providing for cooperative research in education, a proposition regarded with such minimal enthusiasm that it was not funded until 1957. When a one million dollar appropriation was belatedly voted, 675 thousand was earmarked for research having to do with the education of the mentally retarded. Subsequently, thanks in a large part to the activities of advocacy groups and particularly to statements made by such national leaders as John F. Kennedy and Hubert H. Humphrey, both of whom had handicapped children in their own families, interest was generated in reaching out a bit further.

On February 5, 1963, President Kennedy made the following statement:

> I have sent to the Congress today a series of proposals to help fight mental illness and mental retardation. These two afflictions have long been neglected. They occur more frequently, affect more people, require more prolonged treatment, cause more individual and family suffering than any other condition in American life.
>
> It has been tolerated too long. It has troubled our national conscience, but only as a problem unpleasant to mention, easy to postpone, and despairing of solution. The time has come for a great national effort. New medical, scientific, and social tools and insights are now available.[1]

The President was successful in securing a bill, Public Law 88-164, that included broad benefits for the handicapped. In addition to other provisions, this law was aimed at increasing the number of professional personnel available to work with the handicapped, seriously emotionally disturbed, crippled, or other health-impaired individuals. The signing of Public Law 88-164 climaxed the efforts of dedicated professional and political leaders of the previous decade, with additional legislative breakthroughs to follow.

In the next few years came legislation covering captioned films for the deaf and the speech impaired. A much broader development came in 1965 with the passage of the Elementary and Secondary Education Act (P.L. 89-10) with its various titles.

ELEMENTARY AND SECONDARY EDUCATION ACT
(P.L. 89-10)

Title I: This title made provision for financial assistance to local educational agencies for the purpose of operating special educational programs in areas having high concentrations of children of low-income families. Most school administrators are familiar with the provisions of this Title; however, little was done to make provision for the handicapped even though the original guidelines outlined the possibilities of such programs. The reluctance of school districts to start programs for the handicapped under this authority led to the creation of Title VI of the act in 1966.

Title II: Provides for school library resources, textbooks, and other instructional materials. This Title requires a state plan, and the only way the handicapped participate is if those who develop the plan systematically include some provision for the handicapped. There is little evidence that this has occurred.

Title III: The original version of this title called for the creation of supplementary educational centers and services where exemplary programs could be tried without regard to existing state restrictions. Some of the most creative programs operated under the authority of this title were developed to aid the handicapped. This Title was subsequently changed so that it too required a state plan and the state education authority had the final say about who received money and approval of programs. The original concept of school districts having some "mad" money and the creativity that it brings has largely been lost because the districts wishing to participate must comply with an overall state plan which may only peripherally address itself to the immediate needs of a given school district. When the law was changed, it was feared that some of the advantages which programs for the handicapped had under the original authority would be lost, so provision was made to set aside 15 percent of the money to be spent on these programs.

Title IV: Consolidates the general Office of Education authority for educational research and training with the exception of research and training dealing with the handicapped. Authority for the latter continued to rest under the provisions of P.L. 89-105. This Title is mentioned here only because the programs operated under this authority may prove to have an impact on handicapped children although not directed at them.

Title V: Provides money to strengthen state departments of education by making it possible to employ additional personnel who can provide technical assistance to special education programs throughout a state. One of the major outcomes of this authority has been the development of statewide master plans for the development of multidistrict, county, or regional special education programs.

Before the guidelines were even written for the original Elementary and Secondary Education Act, an amendment was made to the act (P.L. 89-313) which set aside a percentage of each state's allocation for use in educational facilities operated by agencies of the state such as departments of mental health and mental retardation. This "incentive" made significant changes in the educational programs in many states' institutional programs. The process also forced a degree of cooperation between state agencies which had not been evident before.

Title VI: This amendment to the Elementary and Secondary Act consolidated various programs which had been in existence under previous legislative authorities. In addition, it authorized the provision of federal funds to the states and territories for the express purpose of improving school programs for the handicapped. Title VI which was created by P.L. 89-750 was the prototype of the basic Office of Education program for the handicapped in existence (in greatly revised form) today. In addition to establishing a grant program aimed at strengthening state programs for all handicapped children, P.L. 89-750 brought into being the Bureau of Education for the Handicapped and the National Advisory Committee on the Handicapped.

In 1966 each state was allotted a basic planning grant for the purpose of drafting a federal projected-activities document and other state responsibilities necessary to implement the long-range federal plan. This gearing up process took more than two years before states began funding local education agencies on the basis of each state's established priorities.

Michigan, for example, received its first Title VI program allocation in the amount of $500,000 in 1968. That figure increased moderately until 1973, at which time the funding level was $1.6 million.

Congress continued to be active on behalf of the handicapped during 1970. In session after session thereafter the Congress continued to strengthen the federal role. During the next six years about a dozen new bills directly concerned with special education, covering such matters as early childhood education for the handicapped, the establishment of deaf-blind centers and regional resource centers, education for gifted and talented, and many others, were signed into law. In 1970 came P.L. 91-230, known as the Education of the Handicapped Act, which combined previously passed legislation into one codified entity.

Thus was the groundwork laid for P.L. 93-380, the landmark Education Amendments of 1974. Beyond authorizing higher levels of aid to the states, P.L. 93-380 was particularly noteworthy for its specification of due process requirements protecting the rights of handicapped youngsters, and for its support of the principle of placing such children in the least restrictive educational environment commensurate with their needs. Additionally, P.L. 93-380 required the states not only to establish a goal of providing full educational services to handicapped children but to develop a plan setting forth how and when the state expects to achieve that goal.

In November of 1975 this important law was greatly broadened by the enactment of an even more significant measure, the Education for All Handicapped Children Act, P.L. 94-142. The new bill calls for a massive expansion of the authorized levels of the basic grant programs, to a possible annual total of more than $3 billion by 1982. Although authorizations are not to be equated with actual appropriations, these funding provisions are indicative of the magnitude of congressional concern.

Of greater immediate significance are some of the positions taken in the bill. First, unlike other federal education bills, P.L. 94-142 has no expiration date; it is regarded as a perpetual instrument. Second, the Act does not simply involve another expression of federal interest in special education programming in general, but rather a specific commitment to all handicapped children. And third, P.L. 94-142 sets forth as national policy the proposition that education must be extended to handicapped persons as their fundamental right.

Summary

With the comprehensive provisions of Public Law 94-142 and related federal legislation, together with the advances mandated by the courts and increasingly being incorporated into state education statutes, the basic machinery would seem to be in place for propelling education of the handicapped into a new era. The handicapped person's right to a quality education is now guaranteed. Though unfortunately there have been serious contrasts between what state and federal laws supposedly require, there is now at least a firm foundation on which to build.

REFERENCES

1. John F. Kennedy: *Public Paper*, 1963, 137.
2. Public Law 940-142, *Education for All Handicapped Children Act of 1975*. 89 Stst. 773 codified at 20 U.S.C., 1232-1453.

Chapter 2

THE RECENT HISTORY OF LITIGATION FOR THE HANDICAPPED

THE beginning of the final phase of the revolution affirming the right to an education for every handicapped child was on November 29, 1975, when President Gerald Ford signed Public Law 94-142, the Education for All Handicapped Children Act of 1975. This law, which becomes fully effective in September of 1978, was built on the public policy victories that were won since 1970 in the nation's courts and state legislatures.

Since the enactment of P.L. 94-142, it has been a central theme of discussion for virtually every element of the education community in the United States. The discussions centered around perceived strengths and weaknesses of the Act and its implications for professionals and for parents. The settings of these discussions have extended from the Congress, the United States Office of Education, state legislatures, and state departments of education, to local school districts.

PUBLIC EDUCATION POLICY

Public education policy is established at the federal, state, intermediate, and local governmental levels by legislatures, boards, courts, and administrative groups. The purpose of these educational policies is to provide the basis for the total operation of the American educational system.

P.L. 92-142, as an Act passed by the United States Congress, represents an expression of public policy regarding the education of handicapped children. Similar policy is represented by statutes that are passed by state legislatures. Other expressions of public policy are the rules, regulations, and by-laws that are developed at both the state and federal levels to provide instruction and guidance to state and local educational agencies, re-

9

spectively, in their carrying out of each agency's statutes.

Occasionally, the intent, or substance of statutory or regulatory policies are challenged either substantively or for purposes of clarification. State attorney generals often rule on these issues. A common setting for resolution is the nation's judicial system where case law is established.

It was in a federal district court in 1971 where the Pennsylvania Association of Retarded Children, in a lawsuit against the State first caused the battle lines to be drawn. A retarded child, Nancy Bowman, started litigation on a very basic principal. The Pennsylvania State Constitution guarantees everyone a free education. How then could handicapped students be excluded?

On November 12th, 1971, a judicial panel issued an order that "no later than September 1, 1972, every retarded person in Pennsylvania between the ages of six and twenty-one shall have access to free public programs of education and training appropriate to their learning capacities."

The decision further stated:

> Expert testimony in this action indicates that all mentally retarded persons are capable of benefitting from a program of education and training; that the greatest number of retarded persons, given such education and training, are capable of achieving self sufficiency, and the remaining few, with such education and training, are capable of achieving some degree of self care; that the earlier such education and training begins, the more thoroughly and more efficiently a mentally retarded person will benefit from it, and whether begun early or not, that a mentally retarded person can benefit at any point in their life and development from a program of education and training. Having undertaken to provide a free public education to all its children, the commonwealth (of Pennsylvania) may not deny any mentally retarded children access to a free public program of education and training.[1]

The Pennsylvania case said that all children, regardless of their handicapping condition, have a right to a free and appropriate education.

Another significant court case was soon to follow. In 1972, the District of Columbia Board of Education argued in court that it could not "divert millions of dollars" to special education, because in so doing it "would be inequitable to children outside the alleged plaintiff class."

On August 1, 1972, Judge Joseph C. Waddy ruled against this contention. His decision states:

> The Board of Education is required by the Constitution of the United States, the District of Columbia code and its regulations to provide a publicly-supported education for these "exceptional" children. Its failure to fulfill this clear duty to include and retain these children in the public school system, or otherwise provide them with publicly-supported education, and their failure to afford them due process hearing and periodical review, cannot be excused by the claim that there are insufficient funds. The District of Columbia's interest in educating the excluded children clearly must outweigh its interest in preserving its financial resources. If sufficient funds are not available to finance all the services and programs that are needed and desirable, then available funds must be expended equitably in such a manner that no child is entirely excluded from a publicly-supported education. The inadequacies of the District of Columbia public school system, whether occasioned by insufficient funding or administrative ineffectiveness, certainly cannot be permitted to bear more heavily on the "exceptional" or handicapped child than on the normal child.[2]

Significantly, Judge Waddy's ruling said that a state not only must provide an education for all its handicapped children, but insufficient funds cannot be used as an excuse for inadequate programming. These decisions affirming the right of an education for the handicapped led to similar litigation elsewhere. Advocates of equal rights to an education for the handicapped have not yet lost such a case.

The "right to education" principle became further solidified through the passage of a number of state statutes and regulations, thus adding to the impetus of this educational transition. By 1972, The Council for Exceptional Children reported that nearly 70 percent of the states had adopted mandatory legislation requiring education of all children who have handicaps. By 1977, all state legislatures had adopted some form of mandatory law calling for the education of at least a majority of its handicapped children (see Appendix D). In addition, P.L. 93-380 of 1974 required that, in order for states to participate in the financial assistance available under the Act, they were to establish a goal of providing full educational opportunities to all children with handicaps. In view of the growth of permissive legislation there have been few recent court suits over the rights of the handicapped.

Consumer advocacy groups and the parents of the handicapped are the real watchdogs of the rights of the handicapped at the local school district level. Assuredly these groups will bring litigation to bear on any local school district that fails to provide the free and appropriate education mandated by the courts.

DUE PROCESS PROVISIONS

The due process provisions in the state and federal laws are at least partly responsible for the decrease in litigation. Due process provisions in the law give the parent a right to request a hearing in an effort to resolve any disputes regarding educational placement. Only the most difficult disputes regarding placement presently end up in the courts. Nevertheless, due process hearings are not the perfect answer. Over the past three years, in the State of Michigan, many of the due process hearings have resulted in bitter feelings between parents and the schools, making mutually beneficial educational planning more difficult.

Michigan attorney Lynwood Beekman, an advocate of rights for the handicapped and the primary author of the Michigan Mandatory Special Education Law, has recommended that informal arbitration be attempted with a neutral arbitrator, before entering into the hearing process. He has further suggested that the arbitration procedure may help preserve mutual relationships of trust between the parent and school district.[3]

FUTURE LITIGATION

Virginia, Pennsylvania, and California have been involved in a different type of court suit. These states have been embroiled in litigation regarding tuition reimbursement for private schools. A state may, for example, commit itself to pay all or a percentage of a child's tuition in a private school. But because of state budget cutbacks or escalating education costs, that state may have insufficient revenue and therefore must pro-rate its financial support. The state then is vulnerable for suits from parents.

An additional problem on the horizon results from the fact that state education agencies must approve school placements for children who cannot be adequately served in a local district. Exorbitant fees are charged by some of the private schools, some in excess of $15,000 per year. The state rejecting such a placement because of fiscal limitation is subject to the allegation from the parent that their child is being deprived of a free and appropriate education.

Other possible sources of litigation may center around the question of mainstreaming versus segregated facilities. The clamor of some advocacy groups has been to mandate educating children in the least restrictive environment. In spite of the existence of many high quality segregated facilities around the nation, a serious question needs to be answered: Does the encouragement to be placed in the least restrictive environment warrant that first-class segregated programs are no longer appropriate? The physical plants in some of these segregated facilities far surpass the facilities available to the nonhandicapped population. Moreover, local advocacy groups frequently support the high quality services provided in the segregated facilities.

The High Point facility for mentally impaired children in Washtenaw County, near Ann Arbor, Michigan, is a case in point. The High Point facility might be described as the ultimate in educational facilities for the handicapped. It surpasses any general educational facilities located within the State of Michigan, and it is probably at least equal to any facility for nonhandicapped children anywhere in the nation. There is little question that the parents of these children would initiate court action if they were forced to be mainstreamed into other types of school programs. Solutions to such problems cannot be found until the term "appropriate education for handicapped children" is defined. This and other questions will remain unanswered until P.L. 94-142 is actually implemented. The courts and state attorney generals will undoubtedly be called on to provide some answers.

Inherent, in P.L. 94-142, are a number of vague areas which need to be clarified by the judiciary. For example, in Section 504 of the Rehabilitation Act of 1973, the United States Department of Health, Education and Welfare (HEW) requires "equivalent but not identical" services in areas such as physical education. Unanswered, however, is the question of the definition of equivalent. Daniel Ringleheim, of the Bureau of Education for the Handicapped, has advised that equal treatment for the handicapped is much more difficult to enforce and regulate than equal treatment for blacks under the Civil Rights Act.[4] There, the goal of equal treatment meant identical treatment; for the handicapped, however, equal treatment could mean discrimination.

The regulation on individualized programs mandates schools to list and provide "all needed services" by September, 1978. It is expected that some parent advocacy groups will test the definition of "appropriate" education by initiating litigation over alleged failure to provide "all needed services."

RIGHTS OF THE NONHANDICAPPED

Another issue yet to surface is the larger question related to children with special needs who are not categorized as handicapped. Many children have "special needs" but funding has largely been limited to the handicapped. Certainly children who are gifted and talented, non-English speaking and disadvantaged, could claim more of these "special needs" funds than they are now getting in most jurisdictions. Bilingual students have the Supreme Court's decision upon which to base their claims. If state courts begin to accept these arguments and the rights of these "special needs children" to an individualized education plan (IEP), greater shares of money would have to be extended in order to provide these children with an "appropriate education."

In the August 1977 Michigan School Board Journal, Frank Wawrzaszek, Professor of Special Education, Eastern Michigan University, reported that "The Education Law Center of Newark, New Jersey, has suggested that a parent of a normal child who receives $1,500 in educational services could bring an equal protection suit against a school district which also spends $4,000 for a mentally retarded child." Wawrzaszek further asserts that "recent actions in California by parents of normal students lacking basic skills may be a harbinger of due process activities by parents of the nonhandicapped."[5]

Robert Gilson, assistant superintendent of the Mentor, Ohio, Public Schools believes that the general education benefit of the Law is that these techniques of individualization will be applied to all children. Gilson cautions that "a backlash may indeed develop."[6] The Michigan Association of Administrators of Special Education (MAASE) reports that some parents of handicapped children are asking why there is not appropriate individualized instruction for their nonhandicapped children too?

Presently, none of these issues have been resolved. But as more parents of nonhandicapped children bring pressure on the schools for appropriate individualized education, the concept may spill over into the regular classrooms. With assurance, more and more special education issues will be presented to the courts in the next several years, and more and more school districts will find themselves in legal difficulty.

What happens as a result of the new litigation will depend in part on how far the courts are willing to go in extending the present nebulous constitutional rights of nonhandicapped children with "special" needs.

Summary

Beginning in 1970 and continuing today, the legality of denying a public education to a child with a handicap, by exclusion, postponement or by any other means, has been successfully challenged in both the state and federal courts.

P.L. 94-142 climaxes the continuing evolution of the federal role in the education of handicapped children. The Education For All Handicapped Children Act represents standards that have been laid down by the courts and legislatures of the country, over the past nine years.

REFERENCES

1. *Pennsylvania Association for Retarded Children v. Commonwealth of Pennsylvania,* 1972.
2. *Mills v. Board of Education of the District of Columbia.* 348 F. Supp 866, 1972.
3. *The impact of state and federal legislation affecting handicapped individuals.* The University of Michigan, School of Education, Ann Arbor, MI 1977, 23.
4. Linkage with section 504. *Education For The Handicapped, 24:*1, 1-3, Sept. 1977.
5. Wawrzaszek, Frank: Toward equal and appropriate education for the nonhandicapped child. *Michigan School Board Journal, 24:*3, 14-15, Sept. 1977.
6. Cole, Robert M. and Dunn, Rita: A new lease on life for Education of the handicapped: Ohio copes with 94-142. *Phi Delta Kappan, vol. 3,* no. 16, 3-6.

Chapter 3

THE MANDATORY LAW — AN OVERVIEW

THE Education of All Handicapped Children Act of 1975 (P.L. 94-142) is felt by many to be the most unique aid to education legislation ever passed by the United States Congress. It mandates publicly funded education for all the population of handicapped children in the nation between the ages of three and seventeen by September 1, 1978, and ages three to twenty-one by September 1, 1980, unless it is "inconsistent" with current state laws.

A major requirement of P.L. 94-142 is that it requires local educational agencies to draw up individual educational plans for every handicapped child. While individual educational programming has been supported by educators for years, the Act mandates it. Further, Public Law 94-142 is in contrast to other federal legislation affecting education in the way it specifies action to be taken by state and local officials. In view of the fact that education is primarily a state and local function, the majority of federal education laws take a "hands off" approach to ordering state and local education agencies how the educational program should be managed. Federal aid programs such as Title I of the Elementary and Secondary Education Act provide grants to school districts, who in turn spend their allocation to school disadvantaged children. The federal government prescribes the budgetary areas in which the Title I money can be spent, but it does not tell how it is to operate the program. P.L. 94-142 sets requirements — it specifically prescribes who has to participate in which meetings and what records have to be kept by the local education agencies. These standards must be followed regardless of what federal money is available even if federal funding is "minuscule," or as low as $35.00 per child for the first year of funding. Intermediate and local educational agencies must meet all the requirements of the law or risk having a noncompliance suit filed by the federal

17

government.

This chapter will not only spell out the language of the law, but it will also define how it was interpreted in the newly approved federal rules and regulations and what both of these mean.

The law includes:

601 General Provisions
602 Definitions
603 Bureau of Education For The Handicapped
605 Equipment and Construction
606 Employment Of The Handicapped
607 Architectural Barriers
611 Entitlement And Allocations
612 Eligibility
613 State Plans
614 Applications
615 Procedural Safeguards
616 Withholding and Judicial Review
618 Federal Evaluation
619 Early Childhood Grants
620 Payment

THE FINDINGS

The introduction to the law has a "statement of findings." These findings are what the congressional committees were told during testimony and in some cases what they chose to believe. Congress found that:

(1) There are more than eight million handicapped children in the United States today.
(2) More than half of these handicapped children do not receive free and appropriate educational services.
(3) One million of the handicapped children in the United States are excluded from the public school system and cannot therefore participate in the educational process with their peers.
(4) Many unidentified handicapped children are participating in regular school programs with their individual

needs being largely ignored.

(5) Because of inadequate services within many school systems, the families of handicapped children often seek services outside the system of public education — sometimes at great distances from their residences and at exorbitant expense.

(6) Advancements in teacher training and in diagnostic and instructional strategies have progressed to the point, given adequate funding, state and local school districts can and will provide effective education for the handicapped.

(7) State and local school districts have a responsibility to provide special education services for all children deemed appropriate, but present funding resources are insufficient.

(8) It is in the best interest of the nation that the federal government assists state and local educational agencies in providing programs to meet the needs of handicapped children so as to assure equal protection under the law.

As the result of extensive testimony, Congress saw a public educational system which had not come to grips with the central issue of educating its handicapped population. Congress was made aware of hundreds of thousands of children being denied an opportunity for an education. They also saw the need for generous amounts of federal education dollars to help the schools of the nation implement the costly responsibility of adequately serving their handicapped children.

DEFINITIONS

Included in Section 602 are the definitions used in the law. *Handicapped children are defined as "mentally retarded, hard of hearing, deaf, speech impaired, visually handicapped, seriously and emotionally disturbed, orthopedically impaired or other health impaired children, or children with specific learning disabilities who by reason thereof require special education and related services."* The rules further explain some of these definitions. *Deaf* means "a hearing impairment which is so severe that the child's hearing is nonfunctional" in school, while *hard of hearing* means "an impairment, whether permanent or fluctuating, which adversely affects a child's educational performance." *Mentally retarded* means "significantly subaverage general intellectual functioning," which also includes "deficits in adaptive behavior." *Orthopedically impaired* means a "severe orthopedic impairment which adversely affects a child's educational performance." This includes "impairments caused by congenital anomaly, e.g., club foot, absence of a member, etc.; impairments caused by disease, e.g. poliomyelitis, bone tuberculosis, etc.; and impairment from other causes, e.g., fracture or burns which cause contractures, amputation, cerebral palsy, etc." *Other health impaired* is defined as "limited strength, vitality or alertness due to chronic or acute health problems such as heart condition, tuberculosis, rheumatic fever, nephritis, asthma, sickle cell anemia, hemophilia, epilepsy, lead posioning, leukemia or diabetes." *Seriously emotionally disturbed* means "a condition exhibiting one or more of the following characteristics over a long period of time and to a marked degree: an inability to learn which cannot be explained by intellectual, sensory or health factors; an inability to build or maintain satisfactory interpersonal relationships with peers, teachers; inappropriate types of behavior or feelings under normal circumstances; a general pervasive mood of unhappiness or depression; or a tendency to develop physical symptoms, or fears associated with personal or school problems." The term includes children who are schizophrenic or autistic. The term does not include children who are socially maladjusted but not emotionally disturbed. The Bureau of Education for the Handicapped's lengthy definition is an effort to assure that "emotionally disturbed" does not become a "catchall" category. Also in the law, *speech impaired* means "a communication disorder, such as stuttering, impaired articulation, a language impairment or a voice impairment, which adversely affects the child's educational performance." This includes "both partially seeing and blind children."[1]

INSTRUCTIONAL SERVICES FOR THE HANDICAPPED

Special Education means "specially designed instructions" at no cost to parents or guardians to meet the unique needs of a handicapped child, including classroom instruction, instruction in physical education, home instruction and instruction in hospitals and institutions." Related services, which also must be provided, include transportation and such development, corrective, and other supportive services as are required to assist the handicapped child to benefit from special education; and include speech pathology and audiology, psychology services, physical and occupational therapy, recreation, early identification and assessment of disabilities in children, counseling services, and medical services for diagnostic or evaluation purposes. The term also covers "school social work services, parent counseling and training; providing parents with information about child development, and assisting parents in understanding the special needs of their child."

Audiology is defined as (a) identification of children with a hearing loss; (b) determination of the range, nature and degree of the hearing loss, including referral for medical or other professional attention for the habilitation of hearing; (c) provision of habilitative activities, such as language habilitation, auditory training, speech, reading, hearing evaluation and speech conservation; (d) creation and administration of programs (e) counseling and guidance of pupils, parents, and teachers.

Two other vitally important terms are defined in the law and will be fully expanded on in subsequent chapters. The term *"individualized education program"* (IEP) means a "written statement for each handicapped child developed in a meeting by a representative of the local education agency or an intermediate education unit who shall be qualified to provide, or supervise the supervision of, especially designed instruction of unique needs of handicapped children, the teacher, the parents or guardian of such child, and whenever appropriate, such child; which statement shall include (a) statement of the present levels of educational performance of such child; (b) a statement of annual goals, including short-term instructional objectives; (c) a statement of the specific educational services to be provided to such child and the extent to which such child will be able to participate in regular education programs; and (d) the projected date of initiation and anticipated duration of such services, and appropriate objective criteria and evaluation procedures and schedules for determining, on at least an annual basis, whether instructional objectives are being achieved." A later chapter will describe the IEP in detail.

Federal dollars can only pay for *"excess costs"* of educating handicapped children. This means "those costs which are in excess of the average annual per student expenditure in a local education agency during the preceding school year for elementary or secondary school students, as may be appropriate, and which shall be computed after deducting amounts received under this part or under Title I or Title VII of the Elementary and Secondary Education Act which would qualify for assistance under this part of such titles."

ARCHITECTURE AND EMPLOYMENT

Section 603 says the federal program will be administered by the Bureau of Education for the handicapped (BEH) which is part of the U.S. Office of Education. BEH is also responsible for teacher training and research in educating the handicapped.

Federal funds may be utilized for the acquisition of equipment or the construction of "necessary facilities," according to Section 605. If within twenty years, the facility is no longer used for the purpose it was constructed for, however, the federal government "shall be entitled to recover" its portion of the cost that was paid out of federal funds. Each recipient of federal assistance "shall make positive efforts to employ, and advance in employment, qualified handicapped individuals," as prescribed in Section 606. The U.S. Commissioner of Education has the authority to "make grants to pay part or all the cost of altering existing facilities" so that barriers for handicapped individuals can be removed. These two provisions — employment of the handicapped and removing architectural barriers — went into effect when the bill was signed into law in November of 1975. Congress has not as yet appropriated any money for this section. The law states that the amount authorized to remove architectural barriers is "such sums as may be necessary." The Carter administration has not requested any funds for fiscal year 1978.

ENTITLEMENTS AND ALLOCATIONS

Federal 94-142 funds will be allocated to each state based on the number of handicapped children ages three to twenty-one who are receiving special education and related services. A count of the number of handicapped children being served in each state must take place each October 1 and February 1. An average of the two will determine the official count. The funding formula is based on a percentage of the average per pupil expenditure in public elementary and secondary schools. This formula determines the total of funds to be divided up among the states. Beginning in fiscal 1978, the law authorizes 5 percent of the average per pupil expenditure multiplied by the total number of handicapped children being served. The formula rises sharply to 10 percent in fiscal 1979, 20 percent in 1980, 30 percent in 1981, and 40 percent in fiscal 1982 and thereafter. To calculate the federal dollars allocated, assume for example the average per pupil expenditure was $2,000, then 5 percent of this would be $100. If during the 1976-77 school year there were six million handicapped children, the authorization would be six million times $100 or $600 million.

There has been a good deal of conjecture regarding why special education advocacy groups supported establishment of a formula which starts low and escalates sharply. It is likely that practical political sense dictated such a formula. Congress would probably be reluctant to support a new program starting out with a cost of $3 billion per year. One hundred million authorization in the first year was much more palatable. Supporters of P.L. 94-142 are depending on educators, hard pressed to meet the laws' requirements, and consumers demanding service for their children to pressure Congress to allocate the dollars necessary to fund the law in the succeeding years.

Section 611 contains a number of other funding provisions. One provision is a "hold harmless" clause, stating that "no state shall receive an amount" that is less than it received in fiscal 1977. Territories such as Guam, American Samoa, the Virgin Islands, and the Pacific trust territories are limited to 1 percent of the total appropriation. The fifty states get their share based on the number of children being served and each state's percentage as compared to the nation as a whole. If the national child count is six million, and one state is serving six hundred thousand of these or 10 percent, it would get 10 percent of the federal appropriation. There are, however, limitations placed on whom a state can count. The total handicapped count of any state cannot exceed 12 percent of its school age (five through seventeen) population. However, no child counted for funding under the Elementary and Secondary Education Act can be included in the handicapped population count.

ADMINISTRATION

In fiscal 1978, a state can spend 50 percent of its federal grant for "support services" or direct services to school districts, with the other 50 percent passed directly through to local educational agencies. In fiscal 1979, this formula changes so that only 25 percent can be retained by the state while 75 percent passes to the local district level. In either case, the state is restricted to spending only 5 percent, or $200,000 of its grant, whichever is greater, for administration. A number of states have contended that this will not even begin to cover the cost of running the federal grant program. Local and intermediate educational agencies, upon submitting acceptable application to the state, are entitled to a share of the federal money that is proportional to the number of handicapped children age three to twenty-one that they are serving as compared to the state total. However, "no funds will be distributed to any local education agency or intermediate unit which is entitled to less than

$7,500." In this case the state is empowered to require joint application from two or more school districts who are not able to generate the $7,500 minimum.

ELIGIBILITY

To be eligible for federal money, each state "shall demonstrate" that it provides all handicapped children the right to a free, appropriate education and that it is proceeding on a timetable to a "goal of providing full educational opportunity" for them. By September 1978 free, appropriate education must be available for the three to seventeen age group (and by September, 1980, for the three to twenty-one age group) unless the requirement "would be inconsistent with state law or practice or the order of any court." BEH's Frank King states that the requirement is inconsistent with the laws of more than half the states.[2] If state law requires education from ages two to twenty-five, then the state will have to provide education for all its handicapped children from age two, but it would not be required to educate those under age two or over age twenty-five.

In one of its more controversial provisions, the law says that the state must "establish priorities, first with respect to handicapped children who are not receiving an education (unserved) and second with respect to handicapped children within each disability area with the most severely handicapped who are receiving an inadequate education." The regulations issued by BEH strengthened this language considerably. The funds "must be expended to provide a free appropriate public education to all first priority children (those previously not identified or served) and may not be used for second priority children until this requirement is met." As Frederick Weintraub, of the Council for Exceptional Children, has pointed out, this regulation actually goes beyond the law and in essence is self-defeating. It would deny funds for training teachers to work with severely handicapped children — the same children this priority provision is to benefit. In clarifying this point, BEH said it was not "imposing any age priority." If the state law says handicapped children age five to twenty-one must be served, the federal priorities do not apply to those younger or older who are served, BEH stated. The state must also establish requirements for (1) local agencies to draw up individual educational programs for each child; (2) procedural safeguards for children and parents (described further in Section 615); (3) tests and evaluations in the child's native language or "mode of communication," which are not racially or culturally discriminatory; and (4) "to the maximum extent appropriate" have handicapped children educated with children who are not handicapped and provide that "special education classes, separate schooling or other removal of handicapped children from regular educational environments occur only when the nature or severity of the handicap is such that education in regular classes with the use of supplementary aides and services cannot be achieved satisfactorily." This is the much discussed "least restrictive environment" provision.

STATE PLANS

The state must submit an annual detailed plan to get federal money under P.L. 94-142. One of the plan's most significant requirements is a "comprehensive system of personnel development" including "inservice training of general and special education personnel" and "effective procedures for acquiring and disseminating to teachers and administrators significant information derived from educational research, demonstration and similar projects."

Private schools are not excluded from the law. Each state must make special education related services available to handicapped children in private schools which have been designated to serve handicapped children. The schools must also meet all federal requirements.

Further, federal handicapped funds may not be "co-mingled with state funds" and must not be used "to supplement and increase the level" of state and local efforts and "in no case to supplant" these state and local monies. In the only exception,

BEH can waive this requirement "in part" if the state furnishes "clear and convincing evidence" that all its handicapped children are getting a free appropriate education. The prohibitions against "co-mingling" and "supplanting" funds often cause a state serious accounting problems and can lead to a federal auditor's suit against the state. If such a case develops, the federal government is protected. The Law requires "such fiscal control and fund accounting procedures which will assure proper disbursement of, and accounting for, federal funds."

Each state is also required to have an advisory council, with handicapped individuals as well as educators as members; to consider "unmet needs." As part of this effort, states must continue to seek out and identify the unserved handicapped population.

LOCAL APPLICATION

A local district or intermediate unit must submit a similarly detailed plan to the state before it can receive federal money. In the main, the assurances, goals, and requirements mandated in the state plan are repeated in the local plan. As such, the district must seek to identify and serve children, have a timetable for offering full service, mainstream whenever possible, and have parents or guardians participate in the planning of the child's program. In addition to the spending provisions covering excess costs and supplanting, the district must also show it is providing program for the handicapped with services "at least comparable" to normal children in regular classes. The language is identical to the comparability requirement in Title I ESEA.

All handicapped children must participate in physical education according to the regulations either in regular classes or in "special designed" programs. In all cases the physical education program must be "comparable" to that of regular students. The Congress is especially concerned with physical education because it says that physical education is an "integral part" of a handicapped child's education.

Record keeping will undoubtedly be a nightmare for local school districts. Each district must furnish the state "such information as may be necessary" to evaluate the program, "including information relating to the educational achievement of handicapped children." The state has the right to inspect any of the district's records "to assure (their) correctness." All "pertinent documents" used in drawing up the local plan must also be available to parents, guardians, and other members of the general public. "All evaluations and reports required by the state shall be public information," the law states. At the same time, the district must preserve the confidentiality of any "personally identifiable information" about any handicapped child.

The "state shall approve" a local application that meets the requirements. If, however, the state, "after reasonable notice and opportunity for a hearing," finds the school district has failed to comply, federal payments to the districts will be curtailed, and if necessary, the state will take over responsibility for educating the district's handicapped population. In such a case, the state will use the district's federal money and place the children in programs "it considers appropriate."

On the other side of the issue, if a district is "adequately providing a free, appropriate education" to all its handicapped children, the state "may reallocate its share of the funds to districts that are not doing as well. These last two provisions place the state education agency between a "rock and a hard place." If a district is not serving all its handicapped children adequately, it should stop payments to it. However, if the district is "adequately" serving the handicapped children, it should transfer its funds to others. In addition to this dilemma, the second provision seems to discourage districts from developing first rate programs with local funds, for in doing so they risk losing their share of the federal money. The National School Public Relations Association states that some state directors have already spoken out that they do not intend to use these powers to withhold or reallocate local shares of federal money.

RIGHT TO DUE PROCESS OF LAW

In one of the most controversial clauses, Section 615, the law establishes strict procedural safeguards for handicapped children and their parents. The rights of parents or guardians "shall include but shall not be limited to" the right to (1) examine all relevant records with respect to identification, evaluation and educational placements; (2) obtain an independent educational evaluation of their child; (3) receive "written prior notice" — in their native language — of any proposed change in the identification, evaluation or placement of the child; and (4) a chance to "present complaints" about any modification in educational programming. If parents or guardians have complaints, they have a right to an "impartial due process hearing" with a hearing officer who is not an employee of any state or local education agency. At such a hearing, a parent has the right "to (1) be accompanied by council or by a person with a special knowledge of their child's condition; (2) to present evidence and confront, cross-examine and compel the attendance of witnesses; (3) have written or electronic verbatim record of the hearing; and (4) have written copies of findings and decisions." During the hearing "any party aggrieved" by the result of the hearing has the right to an appeal to the state for an "impartial review." If the "grieved party" is still not satisfied, they may bring a civil action in the state or federal court. On the positive side, these elaborate due process safeguards may help resolve disputes and keep them out of the courts. They also assure parents of their right to be involved in important decisions regarding their children.

Some school administrators have already expressed concern that they may be burdened down with costly, time-consuming hearings. During public hearings on the 94-142, Edward Keller, Deputy Director of the National Association of Elementary School Principals, suggested that a few, "impartial due process hearings" in a year would more than eat up the total amount of federal aid that a school will be receiving under the law. The American Federation of Teachers has protested what it interprets as unilateral rights. The AFT asserts that parents have the right to compel witnesses, like teachers, to attend due process hearings. Education groups making similar complaints have run into solid resistance. Congressional sponsors of the law suggest that these sorts of problems can be "taken care of in the regulations."[3] BEH has responded that it is only following what the law says.

WITHHOLDING OF FEDERAL FUNDS AND JUDICIAL REVIEW

If a state "fails to comply substantially" with any provision of its state or local plans, the U.S. Commissioner of Education can notify the state and then stop payment of federal handicapped funds, according to Section 616. Within sixty days, the state may appeal to a U.S. District Court of Appeal; however, the law says, the "finding of fact by the commissioner, if supported by substantial evidence, shall be conclusive." The Federal Appeals Court does have the power, however, to "set aside" the commissioner's decision.

EVALUATION AND MONITORING

BEH is required to maintain extensive statistical and evaluative material on state and local programs for the handicapped. For example, BEH prescribed a "uniform financial report" for the states. It must report to Congress yearly giving state-by-state figures on: (1) the number of children by disability needing special education; (2) the number receiving this education; (3) the number of regular and separate classrooms; the number of private institutions; the amount of federal, state and local money available for special education; the number of special educators now employed and additional ones needed. The report must also include an analysis and evaluation to the effectiveness of each state and local program. Finally, the law establishes incentive grants for educating prekindergarten handicapped children. These grants can range up to $300 per child and they could have more important effects on programs in some states than the regular funds because they are focused on improving one area, namely preprimary education.

Rehabilitation Act of 1973: Section 504

Although most of the concern in local school districts centers on P.L. 94-142, educators in most states are risking triple, not simply double jeopardy, if they fail to fulfill their responsibilities toward handicapped children. In Ohio, as an example, State Law 455 requires Ohio schools to provide an appropriate education for handicapped children as does P.L. 94-142. But behind both of these statutes acting as the enforcer behind P.L. 94-142, is Section 504, which states:

> No otherwise qualified handicapped individual shall, solely by reason of his handicap, be excluded from the participation in, be denied the benefits of, or be subjected to discrimination under any program or activity receiving federal financial assistance. Failure to comply with P.L. 94-142 means losing reimbursement under that law only; failure to comply with 504 (and much of its section dealing with elementary and secondary education duplicates 94-142) means losing all HEW funding.[4]

This provision is similar in intent and language to the Civil Rights Act of 1964 and to Title IX of the Education Amendments of 1972. While these regulations ban race and sex discrimination, Section 504 bans discrimination against handicapped individuals in all programs "which receive or benefit from" federal aid. Such discrimination includes school architectural barriers and employment barriers. These issues will be discussed in more detail in Chapter 12.

HEW's Office for Civil Rights has responsibility for enforcing Section 504. Regarding elementary and secondary education these proposed regulations conform in most respects to the language of BEH's 94-142 regulations. However, Section 504 adds a new dimension to the new federal enforcement of education for the handicapped. The Education For All Handicapped Children Act is essentially a federal grant program which like all others, sets requirements for those receiving funds. If a school district or state turns down federal funds under Public

Law 94-142 it would still have to meet the law's requirements, like drawing up an individualized program for each child.

Section 504 is relevant at this point. Since normal children are guaranteed a right to an education, handicapped children must be given the same opportunities, it says. If the Office of Civil Rights discovered the children were not, in addition to cutting off all federal funds, the state or local school district would also open the door for lawsuits from the parents of handicapped children. In essence, Section 504 means that those state and local educational agencies considering not taking P.L. 94-142 funds to educate their handicapped children because of burdensome rules and regulations face the same mandate from Section 504.

Summary

This overview of P.L. 94-142 and Section 504 provides the reader a comprehensive grasp of the essential sections of these laws as they affect public school programs. Subsequent chapters will explore the implications of the Law in greater detail.

REFERENCES

1. *The Education for All Handicapped Children Act of 1975*, Public Law 94-142, Amends Public Law 93-380. 20 U.S.C. 1401.
2. *Final Summer Institute Report*. Michigan Department of Education, Lansing, MI, 1977, 18.
3. *Congressional Hearings*, Proposed P.M. 94-142, 1973, 38-40.
4. *Formal Regulations, Section 504, Rehabilitation Act of 1973*. U.S. Dept. of Health Education and Welfare, April 28, 1977, 1-12.

Chapter 4

STATE EDUCATION DEPARTMENTS: THE FOCUS FOR QUALITY PROGRAMS

THE state education department is at the center of the movement for full educational rights for the handicapped. Since the state has the major legal responsibility for education, handicapped children and their advocates have historically looked to the state to gain their rights. Presently, all fifty states have laws mandating services for handicapped children. Most of the laws were passed since 1971, and some are more rigorous than the Education for All Handicapped Children Act.

STATE FUNDING OF SPECIAL EDUCATION

Aid for special education is now the largest and most rapidly-growing element of state financial assistance to local schools. While a generation ago state aid for special education was unknown in many parts of the nation, it had reached $910 million by 1972. Then, after litigation in state courts affirmed the right of the handicapped to an education, state aid to special education increased significantly to $2.5 billion in 1976. The state share of special education costs currently averages approximately 55 percent.

Along with the increase in state funding for special education, participation in special education has also expanded dramatically. Nationally, the percentage of children in special education programs was estimated at 5.9 percent in 1972, 8.3 percent in 1975, and 10.0 percent in 1977. Overall, spending for special education in fiscal year 1976 was approximately $1,200 per child.[1]

Realistically, according to The National Conference of State Legislatures (NCSL), the fifty states have a long way to go in adequately funding special education. The total local and state cost for special education was $4.6 billion in 1976, but according to state-by-state estimates, "full service" cost in 1976 dollars would be $9.2 billion. According to NCSL's figures, this would put a staggering burden on state education finances. As NCSL explains, the "substantial amount" needed is roughly three times greater than the total projected surplus in state budgets by 1980.[2]

Understandably, educators in the fifty states are looking for more adequate resources to fund special education. Several major funding patterns are used in the various states.[3] Some of the better-known models are: (a) Per Pupil Allowance; (b) Personnel Reimbursement; (c) Flat Grant; (d) Unit Support; (e) Added Cost; and (f) Pupil Weighing. A brief description of each of the models will clarify their intent and use.

Per Pupil Allowance

Per pupil allowance provides an amount of money calculated by multiplying the number of pupils, or full-time equivalent pupils, by a stipulated per pupil allowance. The essential feature of the per pupil allowance model is that the amount is paid according to a head count. This plan is sometimes referred to as a "bounty plan," because it has the potential to reward districts which are able to classify numerous students as special education pupils regardless of the need for special programming.

Personnel Reimbursement

The personnel reimbursement plan typically provides either full-salary reimbursement or percentage of salary payment. In most cases, a maximum dollar amount per employee is also specified. In these cases, the system may rapidly become a flat grant model as individual salaries rise above the maximum allowable reimbursement amount.

Flat Grant

Flat grants are defined as a specified dollar amount payable to an operating unit for any allowable program or service. Many states, such as Wisconsin, have supported special education through such grants, most frequently to provide incentives for school districts to establish programs under permissive legislation. This type of grant is seriously lacking in a rational foundation because the amount is not based upon any defined relationship to the cost of the program.

Unit Support

The unit support reimbursement model provides funding on the basis of the number of classroom and nonclassroom programs and service units. Calculations may be made on any of several bases, but most frequently they include a flat payment for each classroom or service unit according to a predetermined figure for each different program or service type.

Added Cost

Added or excess costs are defined as those per pupil operational expenditures which are beyond the amounts spent for each nonhandicapped pupil. A stipulated percentage of these costs is then reimbursed to the operating unit. Although per pupil costs are typically used in the calculation, the reimbursement is, in actuality, a unit or program reimbursement because financial support is based upon total added costs rather than the number of pupils served. Thus, there is no flat amount paid per pupil, independent of actual program costs. The basic assumption underlying this model is that each district has an obligation to educate all of its pupils from operational revenue sources and any special reimbursement should only be made for those costs beyond the district's basic educational program responsibility. Michigan has recently adopted this funding model.

Pupil Weighing

Florida, New Mexico, and Utah have developed a financial

method which eliminates much of the controversy among education interest groups such as special education, bilingual education, adult education, alternative education, etc.

In 1975, Florida's state legislature enacted a "pupil weighing" system for distributing state funds.[3] Since the cost for educating a mentally retarded child is more than a normal child — perhaps three times more — the mentally retarded child is given a weighing of three. Altogether, Florida has twenty-six categories, with about two-thirds representing handicapping conditions. Various vocational programs are also weighed. Ratings range from 2.3 to 15 and are all based on the measure of a full-time equivalent (FTE) student, calculated on twenty-five hours of classroom instruction per week. Thus, while speech therapy may have a high weighing (10 or more), a child may receive speech therapy no more than one or two hours per week. The district then calculates its FTEs and is reimbursed by the state.

The advantage of pupil weighing is that all state education funding is based on one appropriation. There is no reason, then for handicapped interest groups to oppose extra vocational funding, or vice versa. Secondly, a district can count on being reimbursed at a reasonable rate for the added costs of special education.

Of course, there is no perfect system of state funding. If the state legislature does not fully fund education, then obviously everyone is hurt financially. Pupil weighing will not remedy low state funding. Pupil weighing may provide an incentive to classify children as handicapped and to keep them in special classes. The problem of segregating children in costly special education classrooms more than is necessary was discovered through an evaluation done by the Florida Department of Education after the first year of pupil weighing. The report concluded that there was "a definite tendency to assign exceptional children to full-time, self-contained classrooms, instead of attempting to integrate them into part-time basic classroom programs." Through time and effective monitoring, it is generally believed that this concern can be resolved. The assurances local districts must make to place children in the "least restrictive environment" as required by Public Law 94-142 should help to eliminate the problem.

REGIONAL FUNDING SOURCES

Some states, such as Michigan, Wisconsin, and Pennsylvania, have a level of regional school administration between the local district and the state. These units have taxing powers and, through use of this taxing authority, are frequently able to make it possible for a local district to operate special education programs at no cost to the local school district. This is done by the intermediate unit making up the difference between what a program costs the local district and the amount of state aid which has been made available to the local district. This plan has supplied real stimulus to many special education programs, but many of these intermediate districts are currently having difficulty in levying enough taxes to make up the difference. This is particularly true in states where mandatory laws have been recently enacted.

In addition to providing adequate funding, The Education of All Handicapped bill requires states to provide leadership in special education and to assure that all its districts are meeting the standards of Public Law 94-142. Specifically, states must assure that handicapped children are being sought out and identified and are provided an appropriate individualized education program.

FINDING THE HANDICAPPED

One of the first steps in developing a comprehensive special education program is to search out unserved handicapped children. The years of exclusion of these children has led to the well-documented conclusion that thousands of handicapped children were hidden away, either at home or in institutions, receiving inappropriate educational programs or none at all. In many cases, parents did not even know where to turn if they had a severely impaired child.

The Education for All Handicapped Act makes it clear that

the states are responsible for providing leadership in "the early identification and assessment of handicapping conditions in children." The Act makes clear that parents are not responsible for independently learning about these services and then seeking them out. As part of maintaining eligibility for federal funds, the local school system must assure the state that it will develop and use extensive identification procedures to guarantee that all children in need of special education will be located and evaluated.

Project Find is an example of a federally-sponsored program of active outreach to locate individuals eligible for public school special education programs and services. State Education Departments (SDE) are responsible for project implementation. Six primary goals have been identified in conjunction with this project:

1. to locate the unserved (preschooler's and post-sixteen-year-olds not previously identified), the underserved (those most severely handicapped in each category and not receiving the full service program), and the inappropriately served (those not in programs designed specifically for their unique needs);
2. to inform every agency and individual of eligibility requirements and available programs;
3. to develop and widely disseminate information on the special education service process — location, screening, referral, diagnostic assessment, placement, and review;
4. to work cooperatively with other agencies and professional personnel in developing a comprehensive system of services to children and families;
5. to provide all parents and service staffs with information on normal growth and development, emphasizing presenting signs of mild to moderate handicapping conditions; and
6. to promote understanding concerning the obligations of public education in providing services.

In the state of Indiana a sophisticated child find program

was designed.[4] The SDE first drafted a work plan and asked for bids from advertising and public relations firms. The advertising firm which received the contract helped design the campaign. Training kits were developed and sent to county special education coordinators. Posters were designed for billboards, buses, and other public spots. A fifteen-minute film, "The Search for Special Children," was put together, starring Dick Van Dyke as a modern-day "Pied Piper" looking for handicapped children, and shown on public television across the state. Also, newspapers across the state were contacted to help publicize the campaign further.

The public Child Find campaign was kicked off by a press conference with the governor and the state's superintendent of public instruction. The message was that handicapped children from birth to age twenty-one have a right to an education; and, regardless of their condition, the public schools can, and want to, help. The advertisements asked for referrals from anyone, including parents, relatives, neighbors, friends, and acquaintances. A second goal of the Child Find was to increase public awareness of the learning potential of handicapped children. The intensive advertising campaign continued for several weeks, but a scaled-down version was kept going as a regular component of the state special education program.

STATE TECHNICAL ASSISTANCE

Most states provide technical guidance and assistance to local and intermediate school districts. It is, after all, the state's job to assure compliance with the federal law.

The state of Maryland has helped solve the problem of finding appropriate placement for children with "low incidence" handicaps. Maryland has developed a Special Services Information System (SSIS). This computerized system was designed to reduce delays in placing handicapped children. On a portable computer terminal, a series of code words must be typed in, primarily related to the child's handicapping condition. Within seconds, the computer types a printout of all appropriate facilities in the state. The information includes name, address, phone number, contact person, type of facility, types of children served, ages, sex, exclusions if any, I.Q. ranges, barriers, child/staff ratios, enrollment, tuition, and available transportation.

By holding workshops across the state, the SSIS taught teachers and administrators how to use the system. Child advocacy groups and parent organizations were encouraged to use it as well. SSIS is also the state's prime accounting mechanism for special education. Its data includes numbers of children served listed by handicapping conditions, number of staff, and costs. The data is also used for state education planning and for required reports to the state legislature and the U.S. Office of Education.

Some states, like Pennsylvania, New York, and Michigan, are divided into regional service and administrative regions. Such states do not provide technical assistance directly to local educational agencies. Instead, they provide services through their regional units.

The IUs (intermediate units), as they are called in Pennsylvania, permit a more coordinated and efficient delivery of services, because they bring together more resources, staff, and equipment than any district could muster individually. This is especially important for low incidence handicapped children in rural areas. The relatively small, poor school districts cannot afford the staff and equipment needed to care for one or two children with severe disabilities.

Other states have similar systems, like New York's Board of Cooperative Educational Service (BOCES) and Michigan's ISDs (Intermediate School Districts).

If there is a disadvantage of the IUs or other regional networks, it is that they tend to take children out of the mainstream. Rather than providing all services locally, the IUs often provide them in regional centers. But, if the choice must be made between better services or a mainstream environment, many educators and parents would choose the better services, especially for low incidence handicaps.

MONITORING COMPLIANCE

One of the responsibilities of State Education Agencies is to measure compliance on the local district level. One of the more salient compliance models has been developed by the state of Arizona in cooperation with local school units. The system effectively utilizes "peer monitoring" to check on local districts as well as help them to improve programs. It is called Special Education Technical Assistance and Review Teams (START).[6] In this system, the state hires monitors, gives them some rudimentary training and a questionnaire, and sends them out to visit a district. The monitors are not high powered state agents checking out local school officials; usually they are teachers, administrators, or parents from a nearby district.

The idea is to make Project START a cooperative enterprise rather than mandated compliance. Its purposes include checking compliance with state and federal laws, validating information in the district plan, providing the district with feedback on its special education program, and developing a technical assistance plan to remedy weaknesses in a district's delivery system.

Monitors interview the district's special education administrator, building-level administrators, classroom teachers, special education teachers, diagnostic personnel, and the parents of handicapped children. They are also responsible for reviewing pupil placement records, teacher certifications and special education facilities. In each interview, the monitor completes a questionnaire. They are required to summarize their observations and make recommendations on needed changes before they leave the site. This understanding helps prevent the process from becoming adversarial in nature. Arizona has 225 school districts, many of which are thinly populated and rural. The state department hopes to monitor about ninety districts each year. The information gathered will help the districts each year to improve their programs and will allow the state to better distribute funds and provide technical assistance.

Summary

The four major responsibilities of the states in implementing Public Law 94-142 are fund distribution, child finding, technical assistance, and program monitoring. Lack of resources and experience will cause initial implementation shock in some school districts and regions. Effective model procedures and plans, such as those suggested in this chapter, will need to be disseminated throughout the various states. Through state sharing and cooperation, improved assistance to local providers of special education services can be accomplished.

REFERENCES

1. *Statutory Responsibilities For the Education of Handicapped Children.* The Council for Exceptional Children, Restin, VA, July, 1975, 1-3.
2. Doyle, Denis: *Legislators Action Project.* National Conference of State Legislatures, Washington, D.C., Aug. 1976, 73.
3. Mange, Charles V.: Financial Support for Special Education. *Michigan School Board Journal,* 22:11, 9-11, Jan. 1976.
4. *Florida Education Finance Program,* 1977-78. Statistical Report, Florida Dept. of Education, Tallahassee, 1977, 7.
5. *Search for Special Children.* Indiana State Dept. of Public Instruction Report, State of Indiana, Indianapolis, 1976, 13-20.
6. *Manual of Instructions, Special Services Information System.* Maryland Dept. of Education, Baltimore, 1976, 1-39.
7. *Special Education Technical Assistance and Review Teams,* Monitors Handbook. Arizona Dept. of Education, Phoenix, AZ, 1976, 3-40.

Chapter 5

THE ROLE OF LOCAL LEADERSHIP

THE quality of services provided for handicapped children depends on three basic factors: local administrative leadership, local parent advocacy groups, and local taxable wealth. School districts which have all three of these factors working in their favor are able to provide quality services for their handicapped population. Conversely, districts which substantially lack these three factors are hard pressed to provide anything but the most minimal services for their children with handicaps.

A study by William Wilkin and John Callahan of the National Conference of State Legislatures held that "disparities in special education services can be found in states of every condition, regardless of whether they are rich, poor, urban or rural.[1] Disparities persist whether states spend a great deal for special education or very little." Nationally, their study indicated that the number of children enrolled in programs for the handicapped ranged by district from zero percent to 23 percent in 1975. It is important to look at the differences that account for these discrepancies between the children in various school districts who have been identified as handicapped and who are being served in special education programs.

ADMINISTRATIVE LEADERSHIP

Wilken and Callahan found that "the most consistently important influence on the direction of local special education services is the leadership exerted by the superintendent of schools and his immediate subordinates. When key administrators want quality special education services they tend to get them."

The superintendent is the school district's chief executive officer, and as such has control of the budget. With the cooperation of the local board of education, the superintendent is able to make many significant, autonomous decisions regarding programming and curriculum for children. What then accounts for the difference in superintendent's attitudes toward special education? Wilken and Callahan concluded that the "moral commitment to handicapped children" was the decisive factor. "Superintendent's who harbor widespread doubts about the usefulness of special education programs rarely provide more than token resources," they concluded. "Superintendents who are deeply interested in providing special education, in contrast, often succeed in providing broad based services for handicapped children even when there is substantial pressure to the contrary." An example is cited by Wilken and Callahan in seven rural school systems in southern Georgia. These districts represented many of the negative qualities usually associated with poor educational services: they were socially conservative, poor, heavily black, and rural. However the seven superintendents representing these districts had the moral commitment Wilken and Callahan identified as the critical variable. These administrators organized a service cooperative called the Southwest Georgia program for exceptional children. This venture enabled the seven school districts to pool federal and state money to provide quality programs for handicapped children and to attract first-rate staff to a relatively unattractive area.

Wilken and Callahan went on to state that "in the face of all these conditions these seven school systems are providing special education services not found in much more advantaged communities." Thus, even when faced with economic adversity, strong administrative commitment can help to achieve quality special education programs.

PARENTAL ADVOCACY

School leaders also need to be cognizant of some other forces which help to provide quality programming. Organized parental advocacy is no longer a rare or unusual occurrence. Success of parent pressure on behalf of handicapped children is well documented. Wilken and Callahan stated that "we have yet to visit one local school system which refuses to provide basic special education services in the face of well-organized and widespread parent pressure on behalf of better services." Pressure varies greatly across the nation and regionally among the various states. Generally the regions with little parental pressure provide fewer services for handicapped children. Advocacy groups such as the Association For Children With Learning Disabilities and the National Association For Retarded Children have particularly been instrumental in helping to establish services in many local and regional areas throughout the nation.

Organized special education administrators and staff have also been effective advocates at both the state and local level. The Council for Exceptional Children based in Reston, Virginia, is a nationwide network of professionals organized through state and local affiliates to work on behalf of the needs of handicapped children. Administrative personnel within the Bureau of Education for the Handicapped and in many State Department Special Administrative Education Service Areas also qualify as loosely knit pressure groups. While most education professionals are termed "generalists," the majority of special education administrators including those in the Bureau of Education for the Handicapped have dedicated their professional careers to special education. Many of these professionals who began their careers as classroom teachers have some negative memories of the days when handicapped children were either not provided appropriate services or were suspended from public school programs. The commitment and dedication of these veteran professional special education leaders is understandable and their influence is great.

LOCAL WEALTH

The third influence, local wealth, cannot be negated. Wilken and Callahan found that "in some states, local wealth can exercise more control over the quality of local special education services than all other influences combined." Regardless of the state and federal contributions to special education, those school districts which have the greatest taxable wealth are still in the best position to support programs for handicapped children. In fact, the Education for All Handicapped Children Act (P.L. 94-142) may not help to eliminate this problem. The Act mandates local funding based on the number of children served. Since wealthy districts have often been identifying and serving the most children, these affluent districts stand to get richer while the poor districts may come out on the short end financially.

LOCAL PROGRAMMING

The variety of programs for the handicapped differs based on regional resources and statutory requirements. In states such as Michigan, which has had a broad mandatory special education law for several years, there are few private school placements. In fact, state mandatory special education laws in many cases spelled doom for private schools due to the fact that the local and intermediate districts were given legislative mandates to develop programs to serve all children. In some cases, however, a decline in private placements has in part been caused because the states are refusing to pay their share of the private school tuition, thus forcing districts to educate such children in their own programs. In a few school districts, this has meant "dumping" some handicapped children into inappropriate programs, rather than developing services which meet the unique needs of the handicapped population.

SPECIAL FACILITIES

While there is little question that many handicapped children can benefit from mainstreaming efforts, it is obvious that mainstreaming is not the total answer for school districts. The Hazel Park, Michigan, school district decided to build a separate junior-senior high school for its handicapped children with state, local, and intermediate school district funds. The motivating force behind this endeavor was the district's superintendent of schools, Wilfred Webb. Dr. Webb and his administrative staff believe in a continuum of services and subscribe to the idea of placing each child in the most open environment possible; however, they do not believe that all handicapped children can be most appropriately served in regular education. One of the options in Hazel Park's continuum of services is a separate school, the Marta Jardon Vocational Junior-Senior High School. Dr. Webb has said that the real evidence of the success of the program is what happens after graduation. The questions to be answered he says are "can the children become contributing members of society, and do they have the fundamental skills to be successful citizens?" Dr. Webb asserts that the Jardon School is not a segregated social setting; it provides a "full comprehensive school experience" for many of the adolescent handicapped population.

The modern Jardon educational complex is surrounded by parks and athletic fields. Its students elect their own democratic student government, and write and print their own newspaper. The 225 students are educable mentally handicapped, learning disabled, physically handicapped, and emotionally impaired. "In high school, most of these students would be alienated and withdraw from the school program or become aggressive because of their inability to fully participate in school activities or get the necessary aid they need," Webb said. Many of the more able students are mainstreamed in the neighboring junior high school and regular high school.

The real success of the Jardon School is its vocational education and occupational placement program. The grade 7 through 12 program emphasizes "hands on" experiences. Students reaching the age of fifteen are given actual work experiences in the community and they receive financial remuneration from their employers. Students receive extensive instruction in vocational skills which relate to the student's aptitudes and interests. The vocational areas are varied to include welding, business skills, automotive mechanics, air conditioning and refrigeration, landscaping and greenhouse maintenance, food services, child care, and home construction. All of these vocational areas are geared to appropriately train handicapped students as well as the nonhandicapped. Many of these young people may have difficulty in some of the more traditional high school subjects, but they perform well in jobs requiring specific skill training, according to Webb. The success of the Jardon School's vocational education program speaks for itself. Since 1972, 98 percent of each senior class was successfully placed on a job. Each graduate is then followed up for one year after graduation with additional career vocational support and counseling services.

FULL CONTINUUM OF SERVICES

The ultimate goal for all school districts should be to provide a full continuum of services to handicapped children. The Education For All Handicapped Children Act requires districts to affirm this as their goal and provide documentation regarding how they will achieve it. For local school districts wishing to develop quality programs the following suggestions are offered:

1. A multidisciplinary planning team should be created, which includes administrators, principals, teachers (regular and special education), support personnel and parents.
2. A full-service plan that results from the interdisciplinary process should be developed.
3. An ongoing system of identifying, locating and screening suspected handicapped children should be established. In a compact residential area, this can mean an every home visitation by local parent groups, or it can mean an advertising campaign focusing upon developing awareness in the community of programs available for handicapped children.

Special education programs in any community require a continuum of services, or a variety of possible placement options such as: (1) special class placement with supportive services; these supportive services may be provided through a resource room or an itinerant consultant who serves the child in the classroom program; (2) a resource room can provide supportive help while the child is integrated into some general education classes where he/she can experience success; (3) a self-contained special education classroom for all or most of the school day; (4) a special school for handicapped children, (5) a twenty-four-hour residential program.

The National Association of State Directors of Special Education (NASDSE) recommends that school districts provide the following services: special education programs; nursing services; instruction for the visually impaired; occupational therapy; physical therapy; speech and language therapy; diagnostic educational audiology; social work services; psychological services; adaptive physical education; specific adaptive instruction; music therapy; and career guidance and counseling.[2]

Summary

The day has long passed when local schools should depend on charity from local civic or fraternal groups for the support of special education programs. It is time for local school superintendents in cooperation with special education administrators to supply the leadership necessary to secure quality programming for the handicapped at the local district level.

REFERENCES

1. Wilkin, William H. and Callahan, John J.: *Disparities in Special Education Services: The Need for Better Fiscal Management.* National Conferences of State Legislatures, Washington, D.C., 1976, 23-25.
2. *Eleven Steps for Completing an IEP.* National Association of State Directors of Special Education, Washington, D.C., 1977, 1-5.

Chapter 6

EARLY IDENTIFICATION
AND PROGRAMMING

O F almost universal agreement among special educators is the belief that the earlier the handicapped child is served the better. All children progress through developmental stages, but the development of handicapped children may be slowed down or arrested by their disability. One of the goals of early childhood special education is to help prepare handicapped children so they will be able to attend school with nonhandicapped peers.

Congress has created incentives to insure that states will not erect barriers to early identification and education for preschool handicapped children. Over and above the basic federal reimbursement under the escalator formula, the P.L. 94-142 provides that the state education agency will receive up to $300 for each child aged three to five offered special education.[1]

With the passage of Michigan's Public Act 198 in 1971 and its implementation in 1973, preprimary programs began to expand rapidly in Michigan as well as in other states with mandatory laws. Preprimary programs have taken a variety of forms, i.e. planning, demonstration, and research. Some exemplary projects which have been operating in various regions of the country are as follows:

MODEL PREPRIMARY PROGRAMS

Early Intervention Project for Handicapped Infants and Young Children, Ann Arbor, Michigan

The Institute for the Study of Mental Retardation and Related Disabilities (I.S.M.R.R.D.) at the University of Michigan developed a model program for which the parents were the primary treatment providers for their handicapped children.[2]

Support personnel include occupational therapists, physical therapists, speech and language pathologists, psychologists, and special educators. Justification for the specific staffing pattern was that children recognized as requiring special programming at such an early age would not have academic needs but would require assistance in acquiring cognitive, gross and fine motor, language, social, and self-help skills. While teaching these skills to such young handicapped children had not been widespread, it was felt that taken together the four primary disciplines of occupational therapy, physical therapy, speech and language pathology, and psychology provided the necessary educational components.

A small population of children had been identified through the Institute's diagnostic and evaluation service and had been enrolled in the pilot program. Upon notification of project funding, contacts were made with the area health departments, hospitals, clinics, physicians, voluntary health organizations, day-care centers, nursery schools, and with the public through newspapers, brochures, and personal contact. Most of the children who entered the project at the beginning were both chronologically and functionally at the three- and four-year-old level of development and had only mildly handicapping conditions. As the project continued, the children who enrolled became progressively younger and more severely handicapped.

Referrals are accepted from parents as well as professionals, and the fact that the parents recognized that they have a handicapped child who needs some type of special help is sufficient to qualify the child for initial acceptance into the project.

The program accepts children from birth through the age of four, with any type of handicap, who reside within the regional area.

Each child, with one or both parents, attends one-, two- or three-hour group sessions each week and receives a home visit once a week or once every two weeks. A comprehensive evaluation of the child is performed and a management plan developed.

In addition to the long-range management plan, a set of short-term objectives are developed for each child, and activities for meeting these objectives are carried out both in the group and in home sessions.

A maximum number of thirty children at one time are served by the project. Three separate groups are maintained according to the developmental levels of the children: infant, intermediate, and preschool. During the second year of the project, it was determined that the preschool children, those chronologically and developmentally at the three- and four-year levels, would be more appropriately placed in public school programs or in normal nursery school programs. Currently, the project focuses on infants and the children who are functioning below the level of three years.

Portage Project, Portage, Wisconsin

Young handicapped children need regular individualized instruction. The model project in Portage, Wisconsin, has developed a program of training parents to teach.[3]

Each week, for an hour and a half, a teacher visits the handicapped child's home in the predominantly rural areas of south central Wisconsin, and brings along a series of lessons. The project uses games, household objects, behavioral techniques, and common sense to teach important skills. For example, a child could be taught how to put a button in a button hold; as coordination develops, this can lead to the child dressing himself or herself. All children go through these developmental stages, but the Portage project breaks skills down into small lessons and tasks.

What is distinct about Portage is that the child's parent does most of the teaching. The teacher explains and demonstrates the initial task and then leaves a sequential checklist for the parent. A set of cards accompanying the checklist explains some ways that the skills can be taught. The following week, the teacher returns and checks on the child's progress. Then the child is assigned three new tasks for the next week. An important objective is to see that the child has at least one success every week.

The Portage children have demonstrated the project's success on developmental tests. In five areas of development tested by the Alpen-Boll Developmental Profile, the gains ranged from nine months in motor skills to thirteen months in academic skills — both above-average gains for their age group. Of fifty-one children who left the Portage program in 1973-74, forty-two went into regular schools (some with special help), four went into programs for the handicapped, and five had moved from the area. Before the Portage project, many if not most of these children would have been sent into institutions.

The program's cost is approximately $650 per pupil compared to $2600 for other preschool special education programs in Wisconsin.

High/Scope Foundation Demonstration, Preschool Project, Ypsilanti, Michigan

MAJOR OBJECTIVES. The High/Scope First Chance Project demonstrates a preschool program utilizing High/Scope's Cognitive Curriculum with an integrated group of handicapped and nonhandicapped children.[4] The program prepares children with various handicaps for mainstreaming by providing an integrated preschool experience and by supporting developmental processes. The project also develops methods for assessing childrens' needs and assists families in the total development of preschool-age children.

CHARACTERISTICS OF CHILDREN SERVED. Ten of the thirty-three, five-year-old children in the two High/Scope preschool classes are handicapped. They show delayed mental development, moderate health or physical impairments, emotional disturbance, or moderate visual or hearing impairments.

The project serves handicapped children, identified as potentially able to be mainstreamed in future schooling and eligible for preschool services under Public Law 94-142 and Michigan's Mandatory Special Education Act (Public Act 198).

MAJOR PROJECT COMPONENTS/ACTIVITIES. Children attend a five-day-a-week preschool with half-day sessions. The project invites special education planners, curriculum staff, and teachers to visit the demonstration classrooms and attend seminars on the cognitive curriculum. Parents are involved via group meetings, home visits, workshops, and individual conferences with the project staff. Supplementary services to children and families are provided by community agencies. Teaching staff receive inservice training in assisting teachers in other programs to utilize the cognitive curriculum.

The project's preschool classes also provide a setting for the production of Outreach training materials. These learning packages are produced in cooperation with the Bureau of Education for the Handicapped and the High/Scope Special Project for the Preparation of Preschool Specialists.

SPECIAL FEATURES. The project is based on an "open framework" for teachers, the High/Scope Cognitive Curriculum. This system provides peer contact with nonhandicapped children and encourages the creation of an environment in which both teacher and child plan and initiate active learning experiences.

The cognitive curriculum has been developed and evaluated over a thirteen-year span under the leadership of Doctor David P. Weikart. This preschool program has demonstrated long-term positive effects on preprimary handicapped students.

Model Preschool Center, Seattle, Washington

A group of children who have often been given up on in the past are the mentally retarded. Particularly those with Down's syndrome were often considered hopeless and were not educated at all. However, the University of Washington's Model Preschool Center is showing that these children, with early and intensive help, can learn and can lead semi-independent lives. "We are challenging some persistent myths about mentally handicapped children and demonstrating that much can be done to accelerate the development of the retarded, especially if help is available soon after birth," says Alice Hayden, director of the Seattle center.

The University of Washington also follows two principles used by Portage — the involvement of parents and the step-by-step development of the child. Weekly thirty-minute sessions with parents familiarize them with the developmental stages children go through and with what parents can do to help.

The Washington center is serving 190 children — more than sixty of whom have Down's syndrome. Care starts as early as five weeks after birth. In the past the I.Q.s of institutionalized Down's syndrome children tended to decline with age; this is probably because they were separated from their families and not given early and intensive help, according to Hayden.

Children at the center are showing they can learn, and the longer they are there, the better they do. For example, five children admitted at kindergarten level showed an average lag of twenty-one months behind normal children, but five children at the same age, who had been at the center for six to twelve months, trailed their normal peers by only 5.6 months.

Summary

Preprimary children have long been denied full educational opportunities under permissive state legislation. With the implementation of Public Law 94-142, all states are required to take a strong advocacy role in identification, assessment, and programming for the nation's preprimary handicapped population.

REFERENCES

1. *House of Representatives, Report No. 94-332, Education for All Handicapped Children Act of 1975.* June 26, 1975, 24.
2. *Early Intervention Project,* Institute for the Study of Mental Retardation and Related Disabilities. Ann Arbor, MI, 1974, 3-5.
3. Hoyt, Jane: Portage Project. *American Education, 25:*2, 18-22, Oct. 1976.
4. Hoffman, Charles: Toward a generation curriculum. *High Scope Report,* Ypsilanti, MI, 1973, 20.
5. *Program of the Model Preschool Center.* University of Washington, Seattle, 1977, 19.

Chapter 7

DEVELOPING INDIVIDUALIZED
PROGRAMS

R ECENT educational history is replete with new innovations to provide for individual differences, some mostly rhetoric, but some for the actual implementation of individual educational programs for all children. In order to implement individualized programs, educators have used open classrooms, core curriculum, team teaching, learning stations, and programmed instruction. Of real significance has been the emphasis on determining the learning strengths and weaknesses of children. At the core of the Education For All Handicapped Children Act is the guarantee that every child in a special education program will be provided with an individual educational plan and program.

The basic intent of P.L. 94-142 to provide individualized planning and programming for each child is unchallenged. Individual planning is especially relevant for handicapped children, because they present a variety of special differences. It is this requirement of P.L. 94-142, to provide for these individual differences which will make the greatest impact on the school life of handicapped children.

The necessity for each handicapped child to have an Individual Educational Plan (IEP) will create management stresses for some school systems. Some educators have complained about the expense and administrator time which will result from each handicapped child having an IEP. Herman Sims, superintendent of schools in Madison, Ohio, has referred to the I.E.P. requirement as "a management problem." Without question, local school districts bear the brunt of the paper work involved in the IEP system. Superintendent Ralph Ickes of Canton, Ohio, says that "some building principals are upset with the massive amount of paper work."

Sam Bonham, State Director of Special Education in Ohio,

called the I.E.P. "a rapid evolutionary change, a matter of developing a new technology very quickly."[1] While these same anxieties about the I.E.P. are shared by many administrators, educators are beginning to look at the positive potential in implementing I.E.P. technology.

Frederick Weintraub, Assistant Executive Director for the Council For Exceptional Children, says that more and more frequently, educators who are working with this remarkable new law are beginning to look past the I.E.P.s and past the difficulties of implementation to the positive implications of this government mandate.[2] Weintraub says, "the I.E.P. provides a wonderful opportunity for parents and professionals to sit down and mutually plan an appropriate educational program unique to the needs of each handicapped child." The law actually says the following: The term "individual educational program" means a written statement for each handicapped child developed in a meeting by a representative of the local educational agency or intermediate educational unit who shall be qualified to provide or administer the delivery of specially designed instruction to meet the unique needs of handicapped children; the teacher; the parents or guardians of such child; and, whenever appropriate, such child; which statement shall include; (a) a statement of the present levels of educational performance of such child; (b) statement of annual goals, including short-term instructional objectives; (c) a statement of the specific educational services to be provided for such child and the extent to which such child will be able to participate in regular program; (d) the projected date of initiation and anticipated duration of such services; and (e) appropriate objective criteria and evaluation educational procedures and schedules for determining, on at least an annual basis, whether the instructional objectives are being achieved."

LEGAL RESPONSIBILITY FOR THE I.E.P.

In clarifying the legal language however, one point is clear: The federal government is firm in prescribing how local special educational programs are to be carried out. The law carefully defines those responsible for the I.E.P.: school administrators; teachers, regular and special, "who have a direct responsibility for implementing the I.E.P."; one or both parents; and the child, "where appropriate." If parents refuse to attend the meeting (to be scheduled at the parents convenience if possible), the law says schools must have; (1) detailed records of telephone calls made to parents; (2) copies of letters sent to them and any replies; (3) detailed records of visits to their homes; and (4) assurances that they use an interpreter or translator with deaf or non-English speaking parents. The law explains that the purpose of the I.E.P. is to provide a way for all individuals who are concerned with a handicapped child's educational program to have a chance to sit together and review the background and evaluation of the child and then to plan a unique program for that child. As the rules and regulations state, the I.E.P. must include academic achievement, social adaptation, prevocational and vocational skills, psychomotor skills and self-helps skills." The short-term objectives should be "measurable intermediate steps between the present level of educational performance and the annual goals." The educational services needed by the child should also be listed "without regard to the availability of these services."

THE I.E.P. PLANNING CONFERENCE

The regulations for P.L. 94-142 spell out the fact that a meeting (planning conference) must be held within thirty days of a determination that the child may be handicapped. B.E.H. Director, Edwin Martin, Jr., has said his office will require I.E.P.s on all handicapped children beginning in September, 1978. During school year 1978-79 and in each subsequent year, I.E.P.s must be written or updated within the first thirty days of school attendance. In addition, the planning committee must meet together "at least" once more during the year to review and if necessary modify the I.E.P.

The rules and regulations say that the planning meetings should be at "an agreed upon time and place." The intent of Congress is clear that the meeting should be held at the convenience of parents. School administrators must do everything possible to involve parents. If meetings have to take place after school hours in order to make them convenient for working parents, a possible conflict may occur with teacher unions and their bargaining agreements. The American Federation of Teachers has pointed out that most teacher contracts do not allow for work after the regular school hours without financial compensation. A possible solution to this dilemma is a conference phone call to make appropriate provision for parents who say they are physically unable to attend a planning meeting.

QUALITY EDUCATION IS THE ULTIMATE GOAL

As a nationwide survey by the National School Public Relations Association reported, parents and professionals have agreed that the I.E.P. concept is probably the best way to insure quality education programs for handicapped children.[3] The congressional testimony was supportive of the I.E.P. concept. In the special education community there is great support for I.E.P.s. Pennsylvania, Massachusetts, Indiana, Michigan, and other states have had laws requiring something quite similar since 1974. Warren Jahnke, past president of the Michigan Association of Administrators of Special Education, stated that the Educational Planning and Placement Committee procedure in the state of Michigan has allowed educators and parents to mutually work together to plan sound special education programs for their children.[4] Jahnke further said that teachers feel that the EPPC procedure gives them the necessary support they need from parents to make the individual education program work for each child. Frank King of B.E.H. told a conference of local and intermediate special education directors that the I.E.P. will be a "creative learning experience."[5] Instructional leaders are optimistic that I.E.P. Planning Conferences will become positive inservice training experiences for regular classroom teachers who will benefit from the expertise of special educators in planning educational programs for handicapped children.

AN ACCOUNTABILITY ISSUE

Fears have been expressed both in the communitie; of educators and consumers that administrators and paren s may attempt to make teachers accountable for projected achievement of the I.E.P. goals and objectives. In the December 30, 1976, *Federal Register* notice, the Bureau of Education For The Handicapped states, "Therefore while the state and local education agency is responsible for providing the services defined by the I.E.P., such agency does not violate these regulations if the child does not achieve the growth projected in the annual goals and objectives." Clearly, this means that local school teachers and/or administrators cannot get ushered into court because a child's achievement scores did not come up to the level expected in the I.E.P. The I.E.P., then, is a cooperatively developed educational program, but it is not intended as a binding contract by the schools, children, or parents.

I.E.P. IMPLEMENTATION

The I.E.P. was designed to be the central building block to understanding and effectively complying with P.L. 94-142. Nevertheless some educators have indicated they face a dilemma because of some of the legalistic language of the regulations. The regulaitons state that the I.E.P. "must specify all services needed by the child, without regard to the local availability of such services." The regulations also assert, "all services in the child's I.E.P. must be provided by September 1, 1978."[6] Therefore, if administrators list all needed services and, due to lack of financial resources, cannot deliver these services by September 1, 1978, then they are in noncompliance with the Act. Further, if school administrators fail to include needed services because they know they cannot afford them they are also in noncompliance. In some regions of the nation the financial resources available under the Act will not be adequate to provide all needed services. In these cases, sincere administrative efforts to implement the law at the local level, coupled with parental good will and reason, will need to focus on the resolution of such issues.

James Jankowski, Assistant State Plan Officer at B.E.H., has suggested that colleges of education should include training on the I.E.P. as part of their undergraduate preparation for teachers.[7] Special educators have testified in congressional hearings that the I.E.P. may never "get off the piece of paper it is written on, that classroom teachers are already burdened down with too much paper work." It should be understood that Congress included the I.E.P. as a major component of P.L. 94-142 in order to address the past problem of inappropriate educational services being provided to handicapped children.

The National Association of State Directors of Special Education (NASDSE) has identified some procedures for helping educators develop I.E.P.s and thus implement Congress' mandate.

1. Outlining the Areas of Concern — After gathering all available diagnostic data, the I.E.P. committee should review the child's assessment and list present levels of performance in each learning area, including both strengths and weaknesses. This list should be summarized on the written plan under "present levels of performance."
2. Prioritizing long-term goals — The committee must decide where to start. What are the child's most crucial needs, and what priorities do teachers and parents suggest? The purpose is to set down goals that the child can accomplish within a year. "Care should be taken to not have so many goal statements that accomplishment is impossible, "NASDSE said. In the case of a child with many needs, the committee should concentrate initially on high priority goals and later move on to other areas."
3. Writing Short-term Objectives — For each annual goal, the I.E.P. committee must list a set of measurable steps toward the goal. The objectives should be specific and suggest some criterion for measurement of success.
4. Identifying Services Needed — Specific services should be listed which may include transportation, supportive therapy, counseling, social services, whether the service is to be in a special class, part of a regular classroom, and

the amount of time the child is to spend in each type of placement. The I.E.P. should also specify the person responsible for program implementation. For each service the committee should assign one person to be responsible for providing the service, to assure that the child's objectives are being met. Specifying percentages of time for each service listed, the committee should estimate what percentage of time the child will be receiving each service. Percentages of time in regular and special education should equal 100 percent.

5. Setting Time Line — For each objective, the committee should decide a beginning and ending date for each service. In addition, the committee should set dates for reviewing progress toward the annual goals and objectives.

6. Starting Time to be Spent in Regular Classes — The I.E.P. must also state what percentage of time the child will spend in regular class. P.L. 94-142 encourages, but does not mandate, the committee to mainstream as much as possible. If the committee approved of the stated percentage as appropriate, it need simply list these.

7. Placement Recommendations — The most critical task for the committee is to make a recommendation for educational placement. The fundamental question is: Where can the child uniquely receive the best service?

8. Specific Recommendations for Implementing the I.E.P. — The committee should make specific suggestions for carrying out the I.E.P. This can include appropriate educational activities, resources, materials, equipment, etc.

9. Establishing Objective Evaluation Criteria — For each goal the committee should state how progress can be measured. This means stating specific criteria for success. The evaluation procedure can also help determine if short-term or annual objectives should be made.

Assessment information forms the basis for all long-term and short-term goals and instructional objectives necessary to meet the child's special education needs. Assessment does not occur at any discrete point in time, but is a continuous process. This minimally requires periodic collection of assessment data and continuous checks on the acquisition of student skills, which provides the data for modifying the child's I.E.P.

The Planning Committee needs to focus on such a list of curriculum areas so it has a structure to do some intelligent individualized planning and avoid random discussions. It is necessary that a thorough assessment of each child be done before the I.E.P.

Thoroughly assessing a child's present level of performance will naturally point out areas that need attention. I.E.P.s will contain the level of present achievement in each curriculum area. The annual goals should include the best estimate of the planning committee regarding what the child can achieve in a year.

An analysis of the whys and hows of goal setting has identified five benefits of specifying annual and short-term objectives.

1. Written goals and objectives provide accountability. They can be viewed and reviewed by administrators, parents, and other teachers. With their timetables and assessment data they provide the best means of describing what has been taught and what will be taught.
2. Written goals can motivate students to achieve. Students are told what they will learn and are encouraged to achieve the goals. When skills are learned, students will be praised for their successes, which in turn motivates them further.
3. Goals make teacher preparation more relevant. Teachers previously talked of "poor concept formation" or a "low fund of basic knowledge," but these terms were too vague to be helpful for a teacher. Well drawn I.E.P.'s will provide constant specific reference points for teachers to judge how well students are progressing. Long-term planning also becomes easier when teachers can accurately measure how fast a student is progressing.
4. Written goals facilitate constructive cooperation between parents and teachers. Since parents participate in writing the goals, they too have a stake in seeing them achieved.

In addition they can better reinforce the child's learning because they know what he or she is to be achieving in school.

5. Written goals keep the focus on specific learning activities. Each activity can be planned to strengthen a particular skill. When activities have clear purpose that is apparent to both teacher and child, learning becomes intentional rather than incidental.

The state of Michigan has made significant progress in developing individual educational plans for handicapped children. Of special note is the Oakland, Michigan, Intermediate School District's MEAD project (Modular Educational Achievement Descriptors) under the direction of Doctor Herman Dick.[9] This project employs a comprehensive compilation of general goals and specific objectives. The objectives are broken down into specific components in the cognitive, affective, and motor domains and are criterion referenced. Curriculum areas are included such as prevocational and vocational skills, language arts, arithmetic, motor skills, and socialization skills.

Summary

The I.E.P. is the central core of The Education For All Handicapped Children Act. It is this document that becomes the essential link between the handicapped person and the special education services required. The individualized educational program mandate does not advocate a type of curriculum or methodology, nor does it require that children be individually tutored. Essentially, the I.E.P. is a management tool designed to assure that, when a child requires special education, the program designed for that child is appropriate to his or her special learning needs, and that the special education designed is acutally delivered and evaluated.

The I.E.P. should not be considered a revolutionary concept in education. Many school systems have practiced developing individualized objectives and programs. They may have their own name for it; they may not have operationalized all requirements of the I.E.P., and they may not be using it with all exceptional children. But its foundation lies in the basic tenets of education and exists to some degree in almost every school.

The challenge then given impetus by P.L. 94-142 is not to start anew but to improve and refine educational practices so that all handicapped children, wherever they may be, receive the free and appropriate education guaranteed by the mandatory Act.

REFERENCES

1. Cole, Robert M. and Dunn, Rita: A new lease on life for education of the handicapped: Ohio copes with 94-142. *Phi Delta Kappan, 59:* 1, 3-6, Sept. 1977.
2. Ballard, Joseph, Nazzero, Jean N., and Weintraub, Frederick J.: *P.L. 94-142, A Multimedia Package.* Council for Exceptional Children, Restin, VA, 1976.
3. Savage, David: *Educating all the Handicapped.* National School Public Relations Association, Arlington, VA, 1977, 53-58.
4. *Summary Papers.* Michigan Association of Administrators of Special education, August 1977, 3-5.
5. *Final Summer Institute Report.* Michigan Department of Education, Lansing, MI, Aug. 1977, 21.
6. *Federal Register.* Dec. 30, 1976.
7. *Report to the Membership.* Michigan Association of Administrators of Special Education, Lansing, MI, Jan. 1974.
8. *Individual Educational Plans.* National Association of State Directors Special Education, Washington, D.C. 1977, 15-17.
9. Dick, Herman: *The MEAD Project.* Oakland Schools, Pontiac, MI, 1976.

Chapter 8

PARENT-TEACHER
EDUCATIONAL PLANNING

THE Education For All Handicapped Children Act opens the school door for parental involvement in the educational planning process. Beyond the legal requirement for parent input to the I.E.P., parents of the handicapped have the right to expect improved communication with the schools. This Chapter provides tested recommendations designed to enhance the relationships between home and school to the end that the promises of P.L. 94-142 will become realities.

One of the real challenges of P.L. 94-142 will be for teachers and the parents of handicapped children to mutually work together. There are many reasons why teachers and parents should work closely together. The federal mandate is very clear. The process of developing the individualized educational plan, and the section on due process, *requires* parental participation. The real issue here is the fact that parents know their children better than anyone and have information about their child's development and behavior which is crucial and needed by teachers. A cooperative relationship between teachers and parents provides mutual support for helping the child.

Most teachers of the handicapped have great empathy and intelligence in dealing with and teaching handicapped children, however, some have difficulty identifying with the parent's emotions. Some young parents may have yet to resolve feelings of grief and guilt. Russ Attwater, an experienced counselor with parents states that even children who have mild impairments, with the absence of stigma, cosmetic disfigurements, and the poor prognosis, often have pervasive anxiety which must be recognized and dealt with in a gentle and sensitive manner by the teacher.[1] Attwater goes on to say that, "parents are seldom unwilling to provide help." He further states that empathetic teachers of the handicapped often find that parents become "enthusiastic supporters." The Michigan Association of Administrators of Special Education (MAASE) offer these suggestions for the teachers of handicapped children when dealing with parents.[2]

> It is most important not to dominate the parent, but rather be a good listener. Parents of handicapped children usually have many concerns and need to have someone to talk to. Be a patient and accepting listener. It is important for teachers to listen because they really care. Teachers should restate to the parent the feelings they just expressed and refrain from giving advice. Teachers do need to ask questions in order to get answers to important issues. If suggestions are offered, two choices should be provided so that the parent does not feel that he or she is being directed.

> For parents it is important to realize that special education teachers have a good deal of expertise in working with handicapped children. Building a trusting relationship with the teacher is vital. It is difficult to establish good rapport if parents attempt to place the teacher on the defensive.

> Whenever the parents have a question regarding something that happens in school it is essential that the parent call the school or schedule a conference with the teacher so that a small issue does not grow into an imponderable one.

Public Law 94-142 clearly gives parents the right to confer with teachers, administrators, and other professionals regarding the individual educational program for their child.

Since the passage of the Michigan Mandatory Special Education Law (P.A. 198) in 1971, parents and special educators in Michigan have developed some suggestions for enhancing parent-teacher conferences which have implications for the handicapped.[3]

1. In view of the fact that parents are often more comfortable in their own homes, this option should always be considered. It is, however, often impractical to discuss individual educational plans in the parent's home due to the fact that a number of professionals are usually involved. A quiet room in the school will usually provide an atmos-

phere free of interruptions by other children and family members.

2. Whether the child should be present at a conference is an issue which must be decided with the parent prior to the meeting. If the meeting is designed to focus on problems that the student is having, it is probably advisable that parents and teacher meet alone. If the meeting will be for demonstrating ways to help the child, it may be helpful for the child to be present at least for part of the meeting.

3. Experience in Michigan advises against arranging the meeting by sending notes home with the child. This procedure gives the child an opportunity to provide the parent with the wrong interpretation for the reason for the meeting and is also very impersonal and normally not well received by many parents. Contacting parents at home is usually the best method to arrange a meeting. In most cases it is not a good idea to telephone parents at work. It is a good idea to give parents several options regarding times for the conference. Clear goals and objectives need to be established. It is a good idea to outline these on paper prior to the meeting.

4. Often the parents of handicapped children have had negative experiences with teachers and therefore will be reluctant to come to meetings. On some occasions the child has had numerous failure experiences. It is important that these parents receive some positive input from the teacher prior to the conference. An additional phone call or perhaps a home visit will reaffirm the teacher's concern for the child and usually will win over the most difficult parents.

Parents of handicapped children are also interested in observing how their child is progressing in the school situation. Some teachers of the handicapped are frightened by the prospect of a visit by a parent to the classroom. Good preparation will prevent bad experiences from occurring.

It is important for the teacher to tell the students that a visitor will be arriving, and where the visitor will sit. Teachers should establish ground rules for parents, such as arrival time, duration of the visit, and instructions for observing (rather than talking to) the teacher or children. It is appropriate to briefly introduce the visitor and to inform the class who the visitor is. When students are prepared for visitors they generally act normally. The parent should be advised that when a visitor is in the room it is more difficult for a normal classroom situation to be maintained. Asking the parent to observe particular kinds of activities or behaviors will keep parents constructively occupied and provide some feedback from the parent after the observation is concluded.

After the observation the parents may wish to attempt to carry out some of the observed teaching strategies in the home. In general, parents are not interested in listening to teaching philosophies. Giving concrete activities for parents to do with their children will be more readily accepted. Since parents are busy and have the normal responsibilities of their home and family to attend to, activities that do not require large amounts of time or specialized skill should be selected. It is important, especially at the start, that the parent and child experience immediate success in their mutual work together.

SUGGESTIONS FOR PARENTS TO USE WITH CHILDREN

In choosing activities for parents to use at home, care should be used to select those with which the child is familiar and has already experienced some degree of success. Activities should be chosen that gradually get more difficult as the child learns. It is important that the child not be required to move on to a more difficult level until he has mastered his current assignment. Suggest different ways of doing the activities so that neither the child nor parent becomes bored and the child's interest level is maintained.

The Council For Exceptional Children, Reston, Virginia, suggests some guidelines for parents to use in teaching their children at home.[4] (1) Use physical affection — hugs as well as words to praise your child's success. Even the smallest success should be enthusiastically recognized. (2) Do not correct a child unless the right way of doing the task is demonstrated immediately. (3) With handicapped children, it is important to utilize all the senses. Handicapped children often have one or more senses or modalities impaired — tasting, smelling, and touching are important learning modalities for many children. (4) Establish firm rules before you begin working with your child and be consistent in maintaining them.

The Education For All Handicapped Children Act has begun to have an impact. Many parents have already heard about it and more soon will. Presently many parents of nonhandicapped children know little about the incidence or the need to educate the handicapped. For this reason teachers and parents of the handicapped need to work together to interpret the federal mandatory law and its implications to the public.

Parents generally will find that teachers of the handicapped are their strongest ally in attempting to get better services for their chlidren. Handicapped children should have opportunities to demonstrate their skills in the community. Art shows, concerts, drama, and puppet shows give excellent opportunities for handicapped children to learn ways of self-expression and also to demonstrate that these children have specific talents and abilities. Through these talents the public will become more aware of the educational programs available to disabled children. Many school systems also sponsor Special Olympics* for handicapped children with competition in gymnastics, swimming, and track and field.

Parents of the handicapped should join together. There is strength in numbers. What a few find difficult to accomplish, a larger group of handicapped parents can accomplish. Lists of National Parent Advocacy Organizations are listed in Appendix A.

Summary

Special education has come a long way, and parental involvement with the handicapped child's education program has come a long way too. But the history of programs for the handicapped throughout the country is such that special education had to come a long way: parent involvement in many areas

---

*Information regarding Special Olympics may be obtained by writing to the Joseph P. Kennedy Foundation, 1701 K Street, N.W., Washington, D. C. 20006.

had long been neglected. Parents can and should play a large role in the education of their special children. P.L. 94-142 not only protects parents' rights to involvement in decisions about their children's education, but requires parent input and approval. The challenge is for parents and special educators to work together in the best interests of special children.

REFERENCES

1. Attwater, Russell: *Working with Parents of Handicapped.* Hazel Park Schools, Hazel Park, MI 1974.
2. *Report to the Membership.* Michigan Association of Administrators of Special Education, Lansing, MI Jan. 1974.
3. Handbook, *Oakland Schools Parents Advisory Committee.* Pontiac, MI 1978, 1-18.
4. Winslow, Lynn: Parent participation. In a *Primer on Individualized Education Programs for Handicapped Children.* Scottie Torres (Ed.). Reston, VA, The Foundation for Exceptional Children, 1977, 44-48.

Chapter 9

THE IMPLICATIONS
OF MAINSTREAMING

AS long as some form of special education has existed, there has been an attempt on the part of educators to keep some element of normalcy in their educational experience. Some terms that have commonly been used to describe these experiences are: decentralized programs, nonsegregated class-rooms, mainstreaming, least restrictive environment, and normalization.

The mainstreaming issue, while always a topic of interest and concern, has only recently become a major focus with the passage of Public Law 94-142. This law does not mandate mainstreaming, but it says that handicapped children should be educated with children who are not handicapped unless the nature or severity of the handicap is such that education in the regular classroom with the use of supplementary aids and services cannot be achieved satisfactorily.

LEAST RESTRICTIVE ALTERNATIVE

In recent years, court decisions and an increasing number of laws and regulations have determined that handicapped children have the same educational rights as other children. The law says they are entitled to education according to their needs, at public expense, whether in special or regular classes, or both. These new laws, in almost all cases, require that educational agencies make some significant modifications in their existing structures. The doctrine of the least restrictive alternative originated in the courts of our nation, not in the educational system. It is a common-sense idea related to freedoms guaranteed by the U.S. Constitution. When the government acts to restrict the fundamental liberty of a citizen as the result of a court decision, it must do so by exercising the least restrictive alternative available; that is, citizens are to be denied their fundamental rights to as limited a degree as possible. The doctrine of the least restrictive alternative has been exercised in many court cases regarding the rights of the handicapped to an education. The courts have ruled that placement of children in special educational environments, e.g. special classes, without appropriate safeguards, e.g. due process, is a restriction of the children's fundamental rights.

The doctrine also affirms the right of handicapped children to be educated in a regular classroom, unless clear evidence is available that partial or complete removal is necessary. In the event the handicapped child cannot be appropriately educated full time in a regular classroom, the educational program provided shall remove him or her from the regular classroom program only to the degree that is absolutely necessary.

For some mildly handicapped children this means full-time placement in a regular classroom with little outside support. For some severely handicapped children, this means full-time placement in a special class. The mildly handicapped can be mainstreamed from previous placement in a special class. The severely handicapped can be mainstreamed from previous total exclusion from school. Mainstreaming, then, is a relative concept. It involves looking at each individual child and deciding what setting or settings can provide the best education that is least restrictive of a normal educational experience. It is not a movement aimed at the wholesale placement of all exceptional children in special classes into regular classes. It does not call for placing children who need some supportive services into regular classrooms and withholding those services. It does not imply abandonment of all special classes.

Some handicaps are more receptive to mainstreaming than others. Many children with physical handicaps, such as blindness, deafness, or disabilities that impede their mobility, are endowed with high intellectual and motivational qualities that enable them to overcome their handicaps. Given some special help and, in some instances, modifications of the classroom equipment, these youngsters can readily become an asset to the ordinary classroom.

Children with varying degrees of retardation pose substantially different problems. Some may benefit from being integrated into nonintellectual activities, such as sports, shop and other nonverbal subjects. But the sense of defeat and frustration that these children have might be heightened rather than diminished in intellectual competition with their nonhandicapped peers.

Children with serious emotional problems may not only disrupt ordinary educational procedures, but could also arouse anger and antagonism in their classmates. Here too, however, the degree of the emotional disturbance should be seriously considered.

The development of mainstreaming, which has evolved over a broad time span, is one which could potentially affect every teacher and student. Myron Brenton, writing in *Today's Education,* defined the term as follows: "In essence, mainstreaming means moving handicapped children from their segregated status in special classes and integrating them with 'normal' children in regular classrooms."[1]

This does not mean that all handicapped children will be unloaded on teachers of regular classrooms or that special education classes will be eliminated. It does mean that those handicapped students who, after careful screening, are considered able to profit from learning with regular students, without detriment to either group, would be assigned to regular classes. For some, this might merely mean integration with other students for nonacademic work, such as physical education. For others, it may mean almost the opposite — assignment to a regular classroom, plus special education, as appropriate to meet their specific disability needs.

As educators examine this mandate, it becomes a major issue to be dealt with from a variety of perspectives.

MAJOR CONCERNS

Teachers are concerned with the accountability factor as it relates to meeting the goals as set forth in the I.E.P. Is this a binding contract? How much extra time will need to be spent in preparation and individual instruction time? How much time can be taken from the regular students in the class to adequately meet the needs of a special few?

Administrators, as well as teachers, have been concerned about the pupil/teacher ratios. Should a classroom teacher be assigned thirty pupils when perhaps up to five of that thirty have been placed in the least restrictive environment from other special education disability areas? Parents of regular students are now beginning to raise the question of equity in education for all students. This question needs to be dealt with on an organized and rational basis in order to prevent majority backlash in all of education over unequal rights for the handicapped.

For almost a decade, teachers have been negotiating their wages, hours, and conditions of employment. Hundreds of local agreements have established the structure of the teacher's work day and the nature of working conditions as they pertain to instructional assignments, preparation time, responsibilities, access to professional development resources, inservice education, participation in curriculum development, and other issues as well. Public Law 94-142 is bound to come into conflict with some of these collective bargaining agreements.

Adequate staffing is a prime example of the conflict between mainstreaming and certain provisions of collective bargaining agreements. Adequate staffing provisions in local teachers' contracts speak to two issues:

1. the class size or pupil load factor; and
2. assignment procedures which link student needs with teacher abilities as determined by certificate.

In most school districts, mainstreaming has produced increases in the size of regular education classes without a corresponding increase in support services necessary to assist regular classroom teachers in the mainstreaming effort.

The National Education Association (NEA) takes an advocacy view on the mainstreaming issue but has spelled out circumstances under which it shall occur. Its position is stated in the following resolution passed in 1975 by the representative assembly.[2]

The NEA will support mainstreaming handicapped students only when:

1. it provides a favorable learning experience for both handicapped and for regular students;
2. regular and special teachers and administrators share equally in its planning and implementation;
3. regular and special teachers are prepared for these roles;
4. appropriate instructional materials, supportive services, and pupil personnel services are provided for the teacher and the handicapped student;
5. modifications are made in class size, scheduling, and curriculum, designed to accommodate the shifting demands that mainstreaming creates;
6. there are systematic evaluation and reporting of program developments; and
7. adequate additional funding and resources are provided for mainstreaming and are used exclusively for that purpose.

Some state teacher organizations have taken positions on mainstreaming. The Michigan Education Association, for example, supports the concept of mainstreaming handicapped students.[3] The Association believes that mainstreamed programs should:

1. provide a favorable learning experience for both handicapped and for regular students;
2. include provisions for regular teachers, special teachers, and administrators to share equally in planning and implementation;
3. guarantee that regular and special teachers are prepared for these roles;
4. provide appropriate instructional materials, supportive services, and pupil personnel services for the teacher and handicapped student;
5. accommodate modifications in class size, scheduling, and curriculum design demanded by mainstreaming;
6. insure systematic evaluation and reporting of programs

and their development; and

7. provide adequate additional funding and resources used exclusively for mainstreaming.

The Association urges its affiliates to support programs which meet these provisions and oppose programs which do not meet these minimal criteria.

Further, the Association commits itself to securing legislation and appropriations that will encourage the initiation, continuation, and/or improvement of such programs.

HANDICAPPED IN THE MAINSTREAM

The benefits of mainstreaming for the handicapped child have often been stated, but rarely in terms of grade equivalent advancement. The Maryland State Department of Education tested more than 1,500 handicapped children who were being mainstreamed in twenty-four school districts across the state. In the "classroom reading inventory" administered to pupils in kindergarten through eighth grade, the average grade equivalent advancement of the handicapped children was 1.14 years. This is slightly above normal and "represents a major triumph for handicapped students, who would otherwise be expected to fall behind each year," an education department report said. On the Comprehensive Test of Basic Skills, the handicapped students also did about as well as their peers and interestingly, achievement rates increased with age — from a .7 grade equivalent increase for second graders to a 1.5 increase for sixth graders. This provides rather striking testimony that, with regular classes and supplemental help, handicapped children cannot only learn, but can keep up with their nonhandicapped peers.

CONTINUUM OF SERVICES

All school districts need to work toward the establishment of a continuum of services and programs for all of the handicapped. At one end of the continuum is regular class placement with supportive services provided and at the most restrictive end is the residential school. Between those two extremes exists a variety of alternatives including resource rooms, teacher consultant, and the segregated classroom. Schools need to commit themselves to become more flexible so that handicapped children can receive various trial placements in different learning environments.

Summary

In terms of the total special education delivery system, mainstreaming now occupies a most crucial role. All educators must recognize the importance of establishing a continuum of services for all handicapped students. It is essential that both general and special educators plan cooperatively to assure that all children receive optimum educational opportunities.

Hopefully, we are moving toward allowing children to show us what they can learn in an educational setting unfettered by label-linked expectations. This is one of the truly exciting aspects of mainstreaming. Children who previously would have been limited to a special class setting may now have a real opportunity to demonstrate their ability.

REFERENCES

1. Andelman, Frederick: Mainstreaming. *Todays Education, 65*:2, 18-19, March-April 1976.
2. Ryor, John: Integrating the handicapped. *Todays Education, 66*:3, 24-26, Sept.-Oct. 1977.
3. *Policies Regarding Mainstreaming,* Michigan Education Association, Lansing, MI, 1977.
4. *Assessment of Mainstreamed Handicapped Students on the Comprehensive Test of Basic Skills.* Maryland Dept. of Education, 1976, 1-13.

Chapter 10

THE CONTROVERSY OVER
LEARNING DISABILITIES

A GREAT deal of national discussion and controversy exists regarding learning disabilities. Most troublesome are the many unanswered questions regarding appropriate labeling, percentages, and formulas. The answers regarding the incidence of learning disabilities nationally seem to be related to whom one directs his questions. Some professionals have stated that the problem of severe learning disabilities accounts for 1 percent of the elementary school population. Other sources indicate that learning disabilities number 12 percent of the same population. Often in parent groups, the figure of 20 percent is used. Somewhere between these extremes lies the truth.

The reality of the situation is that we do not know how many such children there are in the schools of the nation. There are no adequate data of epidemiological or demographic nature to provide a base line for adequate programming. At the present time, there is an interdisciplinary group of researchers at the University of Michigan working to put together an epidemiological study of this problem, and they hope to provide adequate demographic data as well. These data, however, will not be available until some future time. The absence of data constitutes the basis for general confusion in the state and federal legislatures and, as well, means that local school administrators have to respond to parental and community pressures with insufficient information.

In the absence of adequate data, some experts frankly doubt the widespread existence of something called a learning disability. Lillian Zach, psychology professor at Yeshiva University in New York, has indicated that the term learning disability is "confusing, fuzzy, and has no scientific coherence."[1] Terms frequently used to describe the learning disabled, such as "brain damage, minimal brain dysfunction, perceptually handicapped, neurologically impaired, developmentally delayed, maturational lag" add to the confusion. Some critics have gone even farther than Zach. Education writers Peter Schrag and Diane Divoky have charged that educators are branding children as "damaged" with no more evidence than "pseudoscientific terminology."[2]

Despite such concerns among professionals over the question of learning disabilities, few professional special educators seriously contend that there are no specific learning disabilities. Classically, one thinks of bright students with high I.Q.s who cannot learn to read. Archie Silver and Rosa Hagin found in research at the New York University's Belleview Medical School that 80 percent of the children who were referred to Belleview with serious learning problems had perceptual disorders.[3] These children often could not pick out a figure when it was embedded in a background design. These perceptual problems often lead to learning failures. One of the most encouraging developments accompanying the new emphasis on the education of the handicapped mandated by P.L. 94-142 is that any child with a learning problem will more likely be diagnosed and treated early. Already data suggests that this is happening.

The types of handicaps being identified and served is changing, and nothing is more responsible for the change and distribution of special education services than the rapid expansion of resources devoted to specific learning disabilities. In Wilken's report, "State Aid For Special Education: Who benefits," he indicates that, in 1973, only about 7.5 percent of all special education students were classified as learning disabled.[4] By 1976, the percentage had jumped to 18 percent, making learning disabilities second only to speech impairment as the most common type of disability.

Because of the growing numbers of learning disabled children being identified, some congressmen were reluctant to include this handicap in the Education For All Handicapped Children Act. Originally, the law said only 2 percent of the number of handicapped children in the school population could be classified as learning disabled, and the handicapped population eligible for federal funding was limited to 12 percent of the total school-age population.

A proposed amendment to Public Law 94-142 (Education for All the Handicapped Act) would have had an important bearing on the definition of learning disabilities in the future. While recognizing the basic tenets of the 1968 definition, the amendment stated that in order for a child to be considered learning-disabled, a severe discrepancy must be shown to exist between the child's ability and actual functioning level in one or more of eight areas: oral expression, listening comprehension, written expression, basic reading skill, reading comprehension, mathematics calculation, mathematics reasoning, and spelling. The following equation was proposed to be used to determine severe discrepancy level:

$$CA \ [(I.Q./300) + 0.17] \ 2.5 = \text{severe discrepancy level}$$

If an eight-year-old child, for example, has an I.Q. of 100, the severe discrepancy level would be 1.5. This "resultant figure is the academic achievement level at or below which the child must achieve in one or more of the eight areas in order for a severe discrepancy to exist."[5] Thus, the child in the example must be functioning at middle first-grade level or lower to be considered learning-disabled.

This approach has heavily been criticized by special educators since both the validity of I.Q. scores and the accuracy of assigning grade equivalents is open to question.

Responding to criticisms which were made at public hearings across the country, the Office of Education thus removed the earlier 2 percent limit on the number of learning disabled children any state may count for funding purposes.

The Bureau of Education for the Handicapped also removed the highly controversial formula which had been published in the proposed regulations in 1976. Objections to the formula had been on many grounds. Some educators opposed the use of a formula to determine the educational needs of a child; others disagreed with the inclusion of the I.Q. scores as a variable, and questioned whether it could accurately reflect the potential of a learning disabled child. The Bureau of Education for the Handicapped received almost 1,000 letters objecting to the formula.

The learning disabilities guidelines, which were published in the *Federal Register* on December 29, 1977, contain two criteria for identifying a learning disabled child that appeared in the proposed rules, but the formula and the requirement that an eligible child must be functioning at a level of at least 50 percent below his expected achievement level have been omitted.[6]

CHANGES MADE

The two criteria still included are that a multidisciplinary evaluation team is to be satisfied that:

1. the child does not achieve, when provided with learning experiences appropriate to his age and ability, at an appropriate ability level in one of seven listed areas; and
2. the evaluation team organized to evaluate the child finds that there is a severe discrepancy between the child's record of achievement and his or her intellectual ability. The final regulations for learning disabilities are part of the regulations for the Part B state grants program for education for the handicapped. Those regulations were published in final form on August 23, 1977 and define learning disabled as:

> Those children who have a disorder in one or more of the basic psychological processes involved in understanding or in using language, spoken or written, which disorder may manifest itself in an imperfect ability to listen, think, speak, read, write, spell or do mathematical calculations.

> Such disorders include such conditions as perceptual handicaps, brain injury, minimal brain dysfunction, dyslexia and developmental aphasia. The term does not include children who have learning problems which are primarily the result of visual, hearing, or motor handicaps; or mental retardation; or environmental, cultural, or economic disadvantages.[7]

To emphasize how inadequate the research is in the area of

learning disabilities, the Bureau of Education for the Handicapped, after consulting experts in education, medicine, and psychology concluded: (1) The state of the art in the field of specific learning disabilities and its associated fields is such that it is not presently possible to specify exactly all of the components of each specific learning disability. There remain strong opposing professional opinions as to the validity of certain behavioral manifestations as being indicative of a specific learning disability. At the present the only generally accepted manifestation of a specific learning disability is that there is a major discrepancy between expected achievement and ability which is not the result of other known and generally accepted handicapping conditions or circumstances. (2) There exists no hard research data collected on a large enough sample in order to state, with certainty, which are the common characteristics of all learning disabled children. (3) There are several theories as to what causes children to have specific learning disabilities. (4) There appear to be no generally accepted diagnostic instruments which can be singularly appropriately utilized with all such children. In the absence of specific criteria for identifying learning disabilities, the Bureau of Education For The Handicapped adopted its (since removed) "severe discrepancy" formula. It said, "children with extreme achievement problems in relation to their age, ability, and previous educational experience, who have learning problems which are not primarily the result of another known handicapping condition, are believed to have a specific learning disability."[8]

While being criticized by some congressmen and educators as being vague and arbitrary, the Bureau of Education for the Handicapped definition does have support of some researchers. In a report by the National Institute of Mental Health (NIMH), "Detection and Prevention of Learning Disabilities," several researchers contend that terms like "minimal brain damage" are misleading and "invidious," because only the smallest fraction of such children have demonstrable brain damage.[9] Such labels, and others like dyslexia and hyperactivity, are usually unfounded and, further, are beside the point, they say. While BEH may have alienated some by not trying to more specifically define an unclear term, it may also slow down the drive for new pseudoscientific labels.

The regulations also emphasize that educational decisions regarding learning disabilities must be made by a multidisciplinary team. The team must use "individual standarized diagnostic techniques," and at least one team member must observe the child's academic performance in class. According to BEH Director Martin, the regulations leave the burden for decisions where it appropriately should be, on "clinical judgment."

One of the areas leading to much confusion among professionals regarding learning disabled children is the lack of adequate research pertaining to utilization of medication for the control of behavior in elementary school children, other than minimal research done by commercial drug companies. Such inadequate research does not seem to warrant the widespread utilization of medication with these children by physicians. There is evidence to the effect that in some classes of children with learning disabilities, medication is part of the daily intake of 40 percent of the children. The reality of the situation is that if there is an adequately structured educational program with appropriate matching of teaching materials and techniques to the problems, and with built-in success experiences for the child, medication will often not be required at all. Medications are poor substitutes for good educational programs; they are often a resort which parents seek when good programming is unavailable and when teachers are ill-prepared to deal with the unique features of the child with specific learning disabilities.

INADEQUACIES OF UNIVERSITY TRAINING PROGRAMS

Another problem with learning disabilities is that the newness of the field has accounted for a lack of a well-prepared core of university professors. Learning disabilities was not so identified until after 1963. Before that, it was a matter of exploration, theory, and clinical research done by a small number of persons. Prior to the mid-1960s, there was no precedent of teacher education in this field, except for small programs at the University of Illinois and Syracuse University.

When parent groups were organized in the mid-1960s, there was a general assumption that all was known that needed to be known in order to provide quality programs and that sufficient dollars would provide the services that children needed. Indeed, less was known than needed to be known about the problem, the situation which still continues today. There were no formalized teacher education programs, nor were there college faculty members with experience to staff them. Unfortunately these new programs were staffed in most cases by individuals who were ill-prepared. There is some question as to whether the universities will be able to produce a solid teacher group, in the learning disabilities field, for some years.

It appears that during the last seven or eight years, there has been more and more interdisciplinary discussion between specialists in the area of learning disabilities and general educators. With the encouragement in P.L. 94-142 to place children in the least restrictive environment, it can be concluded that general educators will need specific training in working with learning disabled children. There is little question that there is a role for both special educators and general educators in working with children who may be diagnosed as having learning disabilities. It would be a serious disservice to children with learning disabilities for jurisdictional fights in this area to develop. Rather the appropriate position would be for regular educators and special educators to develop working relationships which will assume adequate training for each teaching classification. It would appear that in this area there is great opportunity to begin to draw special education and regular education together so they can become part of a continuum of services rather than of discrete programs.

There is a need to study the effectiveness of different approaches to learning disability teacher preparation. Preservice training in learning disabilities is being conducted at different levels. Several universities are exploring the feasibility of training learning disability teachers at the undergraduate level (such as Western Michigan University in Kalamazoo). Some L.D. specialists, however, question whether the 120 hours of bachelor's degree curriculum provides sufficient time for the undergraduate student to obtain basic competencies with normal children as well as children with learning disabilities. It should be noted that most university programs are presently training learning disability teachers at the master's degree level to work as itinerant teachers, resource teachers, or special class teachers. These programs emphasize the interpretation of test results, ongoing assessment, and extensive remedial training. The sixth year of advanced clinical training prepares personnel to work as diagnostic-prescriptive teachers. The eventual outcome of various experiments in training general educators and special educators for the field of learning disabilities may produce a gradual restructuring of professional roles which will hopefully provide greater efficiency in the effective use of personnel in the schools. It is important, therefore, that the schools maintain sufficient flexibility to field test the effectiveness of personnel who have been trained in innovative programs.

Summary

At this point in time, we probably know more about learning failure than we do about the learning process itself. It is very difficult to talk about the prevention of learning disabilities when the present state of knowledge is so limited. Before effective procedures for prevention can be developed and put into action it is necessary that the following information be obtained:

a. Describe precisely specific behavior related to the central processing dysfunctions.
b. Determine the prevalence and incidence of these problems.
c. Develop improved clinical procedures for educational assessment and diagnosis.
d. Develop effective remedial and/or compensatory methods of intervention.
e. Find more and better ways to deliver services to children at an early age.

REFERENCES

1. Savage, David: *Educating All the Handicapped.* National School Public Relations Association, Arlington, VA, 1977. 72-73.
2. Divoky, Diane and Schrag, Peter: *The Myth of the Hyperactive Child.* Dell Publishing Co., Inc., NY, 1976. 12-14.
3. Silver, A.A. and Hagin, R.A.: Specific reading disability: Follow-up studies. *Am. J. Orthopsychiatry*, 34:1, 95-102, Jan. 1964.
4. Wilkin, William: *State Aid for Special Education: Who Benefits?* National Conference of State Legislatures, Washington, D.C., 1976, 18-20.
5. *Federal Register.* March 29, 1976.
6. *Federal Register.* December 29, 1977.
7. *Federal Register.* August 23, 1977.
8. *Federal Register.* December 29, 1977.
9. *Detection and Prevention of Learning Disabilities, Research Report 22.* National Institute of Mental Health, 1974, 19.

Chapter 11

TEACHER TRAINING

SPECIAL education teachers as well as general education teachers are increasingly being aided by new technological advances. Modern supplies and equipment, and sophisticated teaching materials, are utilized in most schools today.

Important technological advances have been made, such as electronic wheelchairs with mouth controls for quadriplegics, calculators with a speaking output for the blind, electronically operated myoelectric arms activited from the child's existing muscles, closed circuit TV to enlarge print for the visually impaired, devices which convert printed words into synthetic speech, mobility aids which use ultrasound to detect obstacles, and mechanisms that translate the printed word into a tactual format. However, parents and educators are agreed that all of the new instructional technology will not substitute for poor teaching. Moreover, advanced instructional strategy, programming, and curriculum for educating the handicapped cannot compensate for uncaring or incompetent teachers. Thus it is important to recognize that Public Law 94-142 places heavy emphasis on a "comprehensive system for personnel development." Although there is general agreement that new teacher training and inservice training must be improved, the question of implementation needs to be resolved.

The Council of Administrators of Special Education reports that within the last two years controversy has been developing in Washington between the General Accounting Office (GAO) and the U.S. Office of Education (U.S.O.E.) regarding how teacher training funds should be spent.[1] The General Accounting Office has argued that since the "majority of handicapped school children spend all or most of their school day in regular classrooms under the supervision of regular classroom teachers, the successful advancement of these children depends heavily on the regular classroom teacher's ability to: (1) recognize their learning deficiencies; (2) determine appropriate methods for correcting them; and (3) find the time and resources to put planned methods into practice." The General Accounting Office believes that the U.S. Office of Education has been unwisely spending its money by training more special educators while ignoring the pressing need for inservice training of general classroom teachers.

The U.S. Office of Education's Bureau of Education for the Handicapped has ear-marked all of its teacher training money to "expand the capacity" of colleges and universities to prepare special educators. The General Accounting Office has responded by asserting that the production of special educators is "now adequate to meet the demand," and teacher training funds are more needed for general classroom teachers.

The General Accounting Office also reported that the school administrators it has surveyed thought inservice training in special education for general classroom teachers was "vital." Moreover, both the American Federation of Teachers (AFT) and the National Education Association (NEA) have identified this inservice training as a necessary condition for supporting mainstreaming. John Ryor, President of the NEA, asserted that general classroom teachers "are just not geared to deal with specific kinds of learning problems and disabilities".[2] Further, he stated, "the kind of training received in our schools of education deals with the normal classroom setting, whatever that's defined to be, but it is certainly exclusive of handicapped children." He concluded by saying that, "if mainstreaming is going to be successful, it is critical that we have teacher centers, retraining centers, and inservice programs available at all levels." The crisis of training regular classroom teachers seems to have progressed faster than support and training. A recent NEA survey of 1,500 members from across the country revealed that for the first time in history, special education problems were among the top thirty instructional related concerns of teachers.[3]

Sharing the opposing view is BEH and a good many special educators. Edwin Martin, Jr., director of BEH, argues that, "inservice training in special education" for everyone is one of those fads that comes along in education. "It's talked about as though you could take regular teachers and, in a week long workshop or summer college course, teach them everything they need to know about learning disabilities, mental retardation, emotional disturbance, cerebral palsy, epilepsy, etc. It can't be done." Martin added however that he does favor inservice education for general classroom teachers on teacher value clarification, "sensitizing them to work with handicapped children."[4]

In the federal regulations, BEH has required states to have "ongoing inservice training programs available to all personnel who are engaged in the education of handicapped children." It is also necessary for "a needs assessment" to be made annually in order to determine if enough "adequately and appropriately prepared and trained personnel are available." The P.L. 94-142 regulations mandate the responsibility for certifying all special education personnel to the states themselves.[5]

BEH's Daniel Ringleheim has stated that BEH has been redirecting money to inservice training. Approximately 25 percent was allocated for that purpose in fiscal 1976 and nearly 30 percent in fiscal 1977. BEH is also "encouraging" colleges of education to include from three to six hours of special education course work in their training of their regular teachers.

BEH, however, has spelled out its number one priority — serving those children who have not been receiving an education; and nationally, there is still a shortage of special educators to work with these "low incidence children" such as the blind, severely mentally handicapped, the deaf, and the severely physically handicapped. BEH believes that to direct money away from the areas of limited incidence to inservice training for general education teachers would be a violation of the intent of the law.[7]

TEACHER AVAILABILITY

GAO believes that allocating money for inservice training of regular classroom teachers would make the inservice training component consistent with the encouragement to mainstream handicapped children. According to the GAO survey, administrators are interested in program modifications and are requesting more general resource room teachers and fewer specialists to work in self-contained classrooms. GAO data indicates that in 1974-75, 51 percent of the special education teachers hired went into self-contained classrooms for handicapped children, while around 31 percent became resource teachers and 11 percent were itinerants who served several schools. In 1976-77 the percentages had reversed. Only 27 percent of the special education teachers hired in 1976-77 were assigned to self-contained classrooms, while 47 percent became resource room teachers. This increase in special education teachers has largely been in the area of learning disabilities.[8]

Many regions of the nation have just begun to identify and serve their learning disabled population. Teachers in this area have been in the greatest demand for the past two years, accounting for (according to BEH) 10,500 of the 36,000 newly hired special education teachers. Another 8,300 new teachers were resource room teachers and 6,100 were generalists. Despite BEH's insistence on the need to prepare teachers for the severely and multiply handicapped, the demand was for only 2,200 new teachers for the trainably mentally impaired and 1,000 new teachers for the severely multiply handicapped. Those data seem to support GAO's argument that some funds should be transferred from preparing teachers for the low incidence handicapped to providing inservice education for general classroom teachers.

TEACHER METHODOLOGY

BEH also has insisted that the best inservice training method is the special education or resource teacher going into the general education classroom to work with handicapped children. Through observation and sharing, the regular classroom teacher can gain skills and values necessary for success with handicapped children as well as learning strategies specifically geared to teach the handicapped population in his or her class-room.

GAO has also surveyed school administrators in regard to the best methods to provide needed inservice training. In order of their preferences the responses were: (1) on site instruction by specialists under contract to the school district; (2) on site instruction by district special education staff; and (3) stipends for short-term campus study preferably when school is not in session.

Administrators also responded to the GAO survey by suggesting some specific inservice training methods. They suggested that inservice training should be on site and under local control; that inservice training should be conducted by "highly competent teaching specialists"; and that such training should include observing special educators at work and should allow for follow-up to monitor how the trainees are fairing. Administrators also recommended approaches such as "periodically cycling" general education teachers into special education classes, and preparing audiovisual aids to be correlated with the inservice training.

Regardless of how the methodology argument will be finally resolved, there is little question that both general classroom and special education teacher roles will take on added responsibility as a result of P.L. 94-142, and these roles will continue to change rapidly.

SENSITIZING VOCATIONAL TEACHERS

GAO and BEH have concurred that vocational education is very crucial for handicapped children. Both agencies have agreed that vocational educators generally are not doing as good a job with handicapped children as they should. Public Law 94-182, the Educational Amendments for 1976, vocational education section, requires that 10 percent of vocational education funds be set aside for programming for handicapped students. These monies can be used at the secondary or post secondary level. This law states, "use of funds expended for the handicapped will be consistent with the state plan submitted under the Education For Handicapped Act (P.L. 94-142)."[9] In effect the law guarantees handicapped students interested in vocational education classes the right to assessment, individual education programs, placement in the least restrictive setting, evaluation and due process. At the present time the federal legislation has had little impact according to GAO and BEH. Many vocational education teachers are excluding handicapped children from their programs according to GAO, and they recommend a concerted effort of inservice training for vocational educators in working with the handicapped. BEH agrees with GAO and urges a formal cooperative agreement between BEH, the U.S. Office of Education, and the Bureau of Occupational and Adult Education.

TEACHING TECHNIQUES

One problem faced by classroom teachers is that the teacher training institutions sometimes disagree about educating handicapped children. Many of these disagreements relate to the mainstreaming issue which is encouraged by P.L. 94-142. The controversy over teaching of blind and partially sighted children is an example. Some educators contend that blind children need intensive, segregated instruction, while others believe these same children learn more rapidly in developing the needed adaptive techniques by being with seeing children. As another example, some educators favor oral instruction with deaf children by teaching a child to read lips and to speak. Other experts advocate "signing," or using their hands to communicate words. When deaf children have parents who can hear, they usually favor oral instruction for their child. Since research indicates that lipreaders only pick up approximately 25 percent of what has been said, it can be concluded that lipreading is often guess work. Conversely, because of the difficulty of teaching a child to speak who has never heard spoken words, it may take ten to fifteen years of schooling for the child to reach a later elementary grade level in language development. However, many experts contend a child who has never heard, i.e. has not residual hearing, will never adequately master the speech process.

To make the conflict even more intense are parents and teachers who often disagree on which instruction is appropriate. Hearing parents frequently prefer oral instruction, while many teachers of the deaf advocate signing. The philosophy of "total communication" is gaining support nationally. This philosophy incorporates signing, lipreading, and other visual aids. It combines the best of two philosophies helping deaf children to communicate with those who can hear and also with their peers. This controversy is fueled by the many alumni of separate institutions for the deaf. Many of these graduates insist that deaf individuals find it difficult to develop emotionally in a normal way when they are forced into a hearing society. They argue that many deaf children develop a healthier self-concept when they are schooled with other deaf children.

In the arguments regarding segregated versus integrated teaching techniques, it is probably safe to assume that the encouragement to mainstream in P.L. 94-142 will eventually win out. More blind and deaf children as well as children in other handicapping categories will be involved in mainstreaming activities. Schools will continue to attempt to provide more and more opportunities for their handicapped populations to have success in regular classroom programs.

Summary

The controversies over teaching methodology and techniques will be settled over time. The question of teacher training will not be resolved easily. BEH and GAO are both correct. There is a real need for many more teachers of the low incidence handicapped. But to neglect the harried general classroom teacher's needs for training and resources could make the "least restrictive environment" clause only a hollow promise. A compromise position could effectively help to resolve the conflict. Some teacher training monies need to be allocated for retraining general classroom and vocational teachers while other funds will be needed to increase the number of teachers for the "low incidence" handicapped.

REFERENCES

1. HEW Responds to GAO Report. *CASE Newsletter, Council for Administrators of Special Education, 18*:4,5, Summer, 1977.
2. Ryor, John: Integrating the Handicapped. *Todays Education, 66*:3, 27, Sept.-Oct., 1977.
3. Andelman, Frederick et al.: Mainstreaming. *Todays Education, 65*:2, 18-19, March-April, 1976.
4. Martin, Edwin: Some thoughts on mainstreaming. *Exceptional Child, 41*:3, 150-154, Nov., 1974.
5. *Federal Register.* Aug. 23, 1977.
6. *Placement of Special Education Students, Final Institute Report.* Michigan Department of Education, Lansing MI, Sept., 1977, 16.
7. Summary of GAO Report to Congress. *CASE Newsletter, Council for Administrators of Special Education, 18*:4, 3.
8. *Report to Congress: Need to Redirect Federal Programs for Training Educators for the Handicapped.* Government Accounting Office, Washington, D.C., 1977, 2-21.
9. *Federal Register.* Aug. 23, 1977.

Chapter 12

NEW OPPORTUNITIES FOR
THE HANDICAPPED

IN 1973, Section 504 of the Rehabilitation Act
was passed into law. It was not until April 28, 1977, that the
Secretary of Health, Education and Welfare, Joseph A. Cali-
fano, issued the formal regulations pursuant to this act. His
accompanying message reads as follows:

> Today I am issuing a regulation, pursuant to Section 504 of
> the Rehabilitation Act of 1973, that will open a new world of
> equal opportunity for more than 35 million handicapped
> Americans — the blind, the deaf, persons confined to wheel
> chairs, the mentally ill or retarded, and those with other
> handicaps.

> The 504 Regulation attacks the discrimination, the de-
> meaning practices and the injustices that have afflicted the
> nation's handicapped citizens. It reflects the recognition of
> the Congress that most handicapped persons can lead proud
> and productive lives, despite their disability. It will usher in a
> new era of equality for handicapped individuals in which
> unfair barriers to self-sufficiency and decent treatment will
> begin to fall before the force of law.[1]

This monumental law prohibits discrimination on the basis
of physical or mental handicap in every federally-assisted program or activity in the country.

Section 504 states that: "No otherwise qualified handicapped
individual in the United States . . . shall, solely by reason of his
handicap, be excluded from the participation in, be denied the
benefits of, or be subjected to discrimination under any program or activity receiving federal financial assistance."

The term handicap includes such diseases or conditions as
speech, hearing, visual, and orthopedic impairments; cerebral
palsy, epilepsy, muscular dystrophy, multiple sclerosis, cancer,

96

diabetes, heart disease, mental retardation, emotional illness; and specific learning disabilities, such as perceptual handicaps, dyslexia, minimal brain dysfunction, and developmental aphasia.

CHANGING SCHOOL ARCHITECTURE

The regulation provides that programs must be accessible to handicapped persons. It does not require that every building or part of a building must be accessible, but the program as a whole must be accessible. Structural changes to make the program accessible must be made only if alternatives, such as reassignment of classes or home visits, are not possible. The intent is to make all benefits or services available to handicapped persons as soon as possible. Institutions are given three years to complete structural changes to their physical plants; nonstructural changes must be made in sixty days.

MANDATE TO REMOVE BARRIERS

Section 504 regulations specifically prohibit architectual barriers in new or old school buildings from standing in the way of a handicapped person's educational opportunity. A school "program or activity, when viewed in its entirety, must be readily accessible to handicapped persons." The key phrase is "in its entirety"; thus, not every classroom, or even every building, need be absolutely barrier free. If, for example, a high school student who is not ambulatory wishes to take biology, the school is required to make a biology laboratory available. Rather than installing costly elevators in an old building, the school could convert a first floor classroom to a biology laboratory. Courses like art, music, and physical education must also be offered to handicapped students, even if equipment and facilities must be redesigned to meet their needs. The Office of Civil Rights estimates the cost of bringing all existing education buildings into compliance at between $150 and $330 million. The federal handicapped law (P.L. 94-142) specifically authorizes grants to schools to eliminate architectural barriers, but, so far, the Carter Administration has not requested any funds for this purpose. One avenue worth following is the federal Public Works Capital Investment program. Begun as an antirecessionary job creation program, it specifically lists schools as eligible recipients, and necessary renovations to eliminate architectural barriers would probably rate high among the applications for funds.

Perhaps, too, the potential cost of renovation has been drastically overestimated. An (EFL) Educational Facilities Laboratory report, "Architectural Accessibility," found many examples where the true cost of renovation was far less than the first "hasty" estimates had suggested. A study by the National League of Cities concluded that the extra cost for accessibility for new buildings was 0.1 to 0.5 percent of the building cost, and about 1 percent to renovate an existing facility.[2] An HEW handbook, "Design of Barrier-Free Facilities," says, "In most new construction, the additional cost of making a facility barrier-free is negligible and should not interfere with application of the standards. The remodeling of existing structures does involve additional costs which vary widely. However, the value to society of having the disabled population more fully independent and usefully employed outweights the cost of making facilities accessible."[3]

A U.S. General Accounting Office study also found that the cost of accessibility was often negligible.[4] Its report concludes: "When compared to total project costs, the current cost of altering buildings to comply with American National Standards Institute standards is relatively small. The percentages range from .06 percent to 2.4 percent of the project cost. However, the cost is even less when accessibility features are incorporated into the original construction program. In all instances, they amounted to less than 1 percent of total project cost."

EMPLOYMENT PROVISIONS

The general employment provisions are that employers may not refuse to hire or promote handicapped persons solely because of their disability. Reasonable accommodation may also have to be made to the person's handicap where needed.

For employees as well as students or patients, accessibility is a primary necessity. Examples of reasonable accommodations might include a cassette recorder for a blind employee, changes in the physical location of the task to be performed, or similar actions. Under certain circumstances, an employer might find it necessary to make more extensive changes. The size and type of employing agency and the cost involved are considerations in determining undue hardship.

Failure to employ or promote an employee who is unqualified or who cannot be helped by reasonable accommodation is not discrimination. However, an employer may not reject an applicant simply because reasonable accommodation is necessary.

Pre-employment physical examinations may not be required and pre-employment inquiry cannot be made about a person's handicapping condition although employers may ask about an applicant's ability to perform job-related functions. Employers may make an offer of employment conditional on medical examination as long as the examination is required of all employees, and no one is disqualified on the basis of a physical condition that is not job related.

Section 504 of the Rehabilitation Act of 1973 actually serves to enforce P.L. 94-142. The Office of Civil Rights (OCR) monitors compliance with Section 504. If OCR finds a school district in noncompliance with Section 504 the district could have all federal funds cut off.

Summary

Section 504 has helped to strip away the barriers to opportunity for the handicapped. For too long, the handicapped have been discriminated against in both education and employment. Now this neglected segment of society may more fully take their place in the mainstream of life.

REFERENCES

1. *Federal Register.* April 28, 1977.
2. *Architectural Accessibility.* Educational Facilities Laboratory, New York, 1977, 3-6.
3. *Design of Barrier-Free Facilities.* U.S. Department of Health, Education and Welfare, Washington, D.C., 1977, 18-21.
4. *Architectural Accessibility Cost Projections.* General Accounting Office, Washington, D.C., 1977, 1-8.

EPILOGUE

THE Education for All Handicapped Children Act of 1975, P.L. 94-142 is not revolutionary in terms of what it requires. It is revolutionary in terms of a new role for the federal government. As depicted in Chapters 1 and 2, P.L. 94-142 represents the standards that have over the past eight years been laid down by the courts, legislatures, and other policy bodies of our country.

In this century we have witnessed educational services for the handicapped go full cycle, from the educational community paying little attention to the needs of the handicapped to the implementation of comprehensive programs, and now to an emphasis on returning handicapped children to regular classrooms. However, there should be major differences between today's programming and what was prevalent fifty years ago. Even though the emphasis in P.L. 94-142 is on returning handicapped children to the regular classroom, appropriate supportive services are a necessity. For educators to allow children to be "mainstreamed" without the support services which are essential for success will negate the intent of the law.

The authors believe that the concern shown for the handicapped is one measure of the level of civilization in a country. Nations which must be primarily concerned with feeding their hungry masses are able to make little effort toward serving the handicapped. The Education for All Handicapped Act affirms this nation's belief in the fundamental civil rights of every handicapped person.

P.L. 94-142 will only be effective if professional practioners and parent-consumers make it work by using some of the procedures set forth in this book.

101

Appendix A

ORGANIZATIONS AND AGENCIES CONCERNED WITH EXCEPTIONAL PERSONS

Alexander Graham Bell Association for the Deaf, Inc.
3417 Volta Place
Washington DC 20007

American Association for Gifted Children
15 Gramercy Park
New York NY 10003

American Association on Mental Deficiency
5201 Connecticut Avenue, NW
Washington DC 20015

American Foundation for the Blind
15 West Sixteenth Street
New York NY 10011

American Printing House for the Blind
P.O. Box 6085
Louisville KY 40206

American Psychological Association
1200 Seventeenth Street, NW
Washington DC 20036

American Speech and Hearing Association
9030 Old Georgetown Road
Washington DC 20014

ARC Reprinter's Corporation*
21 Northampton Street
Buffalo NY 14209

Association for Children with Learning Disabilities
5225 Grace Street
Pittsburgh PA 15236

Association for the Aid of Crippled Children
345 East 46th Street
New York NY 10017

Association for the Education of the Visually Handicapped
919 Walnut, Fourth Floor
Philadelphia PA 19107

Association of Rehabilitation Facilities
5530 Wisconsin Avenue
Washington DC 20015

Bell & Howell Company*
Duopage Department, Micro Photo Division
Old Mansfield Road
Wooster OH 44619

Braille Circulating Library
2823 West Grace Street
Richmond VA 23221

*Suppliers of type enlargement materials

103

Clearinghouse on Programs and
Research in Child Abuse and
Neglect
Herner and Company
2100 M Street, NW, Suite 316
Washington DC 20037

Closer Look
National Information Center for
the Handicapped
1201 Sixteenth Street, NW
Washington DC 20037

The Council for Exceptional
Children
1920 Association Drive
Reston VA 22091

Crane Duplicating Service*
P.O. Box 487
Barnstable MA 02630

Dakota Microfilm Services, Inc.*
North Central Office
501 North Dakota Street
St. Paul MN 55103

Division for the Blind and Physi-
cally Handicapped
Library of Congress
Washington DC 20542

Eye Gate House, Inc.
146-01 Archer Avenue
Jamaica NY 11435

Gifted Child Society, Inc.
59 Glen Gray Road
Oakland NJ 07436

Large Type Books in Print
R.R. Bowker Company
1180 Avenue of the Americas
New York NY 10036

Library Reproduction Service*
1977 South Los Angeles Street
Los Angeles CA 90011

Muscular Dystrophy Association
810 Seventh Avenue
New York NY 10019

National Association for Creative
Children and Adults
8080 Springvalley Drive
Cincinnati OH 45236

National Association of the Deaf
814 Thayer Avenue
Silver Spring MD 20910

National Association for Retarded Children
2709 Avenue E East
Arlington TX 76011

National Association for the Visually Handicapped
3201 Balboa Street
San Francisco CA 94121

National Braille Press
88 St. Stephen Street
Boston MA 02115

National Center on Educational
Media and Materials for the
Handicapped
The Ohio State University
Columbus OH 43210

National Easter Seal Society for
Crippled Children and Adults
2023 West Ogden Avenue
Chicago IL 60612

---

*Suppliers of type enlargement materials

National Foundation
March of Dimes
Division of Health Information
and School Relations
1275 Mamaroneck Avenue
White Plains NY 10605

National Rehabilitation Association
1522 K Street, NW
Washington DC 20005

National Society for Autistic Children
169 Tampa Avenue
Albany NY 12208

National Society for Autistic Children
Information & Referral Service
306 - 31st Street
Huntington WV 25702

Orton Society, Inc.
8415 Bellona Lane
Baltimore MD 21204

Recording for the Blind, Inc.
215 East 58th Street
New York NY 10022

Singer Education and Training Products
Society for Visual Education, Inc.
1345 Diversey Parkway
Chicago IL 60614

United Cerebral Palsy Association
Program Department
66 East 34th Street
New York NY 10016

We Are People First
P.O. Box 5208
Salem OR 97304

FEDERALLY SPONSORED LEARNING RESOURCE CENTERS

IN 1974 the Bureau of Education for the Handicapped awarded contracts to twenty-six regional contractors to form the nationwide Learning Resource Center (LRC) network. Thirteen contracts were awarded to Regional Resource Centers (RRCs) and thirteen to Area Learning Resource Centers (ALRCs). The RRC network is designed to stimulate, reinforce, and guide individual states and local agencies in their efforts to reach the 1980 BEH goal: to provide an appropriate education for every handicapped child.

Whereas coordination between the RRCs and ALRCs is provided in the Learning Resource Center concept, each program has specific responsibilities. RRCs are basically responsible for appraisal of and programming for handicapped children, whereas the ALRCs are accountable for the development of materials, media, and educational technology services to those identified as needing special intervention.

To appreciate fully this rather complex system one will need to utilize the services that are available. A listing of LRC contractors by region is provided so that educators and others interested in the services may contact the office in their area for further information.

LEARNING RESOURCE CENTER NETWORK

Regional Resource Center	*States Served*
Northwest Regional Resource Center	Alaska, Hawaii,
Project Director	Samoa, Guam,
University of Oregon	Trust Territory,
Clinical Services Bldg., Third Floor	WA, ID,
Eugene, OR 97403	OR, MT,
	WY

California Regional Resource Center CA
Project Director
1031 S. Broadway, Suite 623
Los Angeles, CA 90007

Southwest Regional Resource Center NV, UT,
Project Director CO, AZ,
2363 Foot Hill Dr., Suite G NM, B.I.A.
Salt Lake City, UT 84109 Schools

Midwest Regional Resource Center ND, SD,
Project Director NE, KS,
Drake University OK, IA,
1332 26th St. MO, AR
Des Moines, IA 50311

Texas Regional Resource Center TX
Project Director
Texas Education Agency
201 E. 11th St.
Austin, TX 78701

Great Lakes Regional Resource Center MN, WI
Project Director MI, IN
Wisconsin State Department of
    Public Instruction
126 Langdon St.
Madison, WI 53702

Illinois Regional Resource Center IL
Project Director
Peoria Public School District
3202 N. Wisconsin Ave.
Peoria, IL 61603

Ohio Regional Resource Center OH
Project Director
Ohio State Department of Education
Division of Special Education
933 High St.
Worthington, OH 43085

Northeast Regional Resource Center ME, VT
Project Director NH, MA
384 Stockton St. RI, CT
Highstown, NJ 08520 NJ

New York Regional Resource Center   NY
Project Director
City University of New York
144 W. 125th St.
New York, NY 10027

Pennsylvania Regional Resource Center   PA
Project Director
443 S. Gulph Rd.
King of Prussia, PA 19406

Mid-East Regional Resource Center   DE, DC
Project Director   MD, VA
1901 Pennsylvania Ave., N.W.   WV, KY
Washington, DC 20036   TN, NC

Southeast Regional Resource Center   LA, MS
Project Director   AL, GA
Auburn University at Montgomery   SC, FL
Montgomery, AL 36109   P.R., Virgin Is.

Coordinating Office for the Area Regional Resource Centers
CORRC Project
Project Director
Bradley Hall
University of Kentucky
Lexington, KY 40506

Area Learning Resource Center   States served
Northwest Area Learning Resource   AK, HI
Project Director   Trust Territory,
University of Oregon   Guam, Samoa,
Clinical Services Bldg., Third floor   WA, OR
Eugene, OR 97403   WY

California Area Learning Resource Center   CA
Project Director
1031 S. Broadway
Suite 623
Los Angeles, CA 90007

Southwest Area Learning Resource Center   NV, UT
Project Director   CO, AZ
New Mexico State University   NM, B.I.A.
Box 3AW   Schools
Las Cruces, NM 88003

Midwest Area Learning Resource Center — ND, SD
Project Director — IA, NE,
114 Second Ave. — KS, OK,
Coralville, IA 52241 — MO, AR

Texas Area Learning Resource Center — TX
Project Director
Texas Area Learning Resource Center
2613 Wichita St.
Austin, TX 78701

Great Lakes Area Learning Resource Center — MN, WI
Project Director — MI, IN
Michigan Department of Education
P.O. Box 420
Lansing, MI 48902

Illinois Area Learning Resource Center — IL
Project Director
1020 S. Spring St.
Springfield, IL 62706

Ohio Area Learning Resource Center — OH
Project Director
Ohio Division of Special Education
933 High St.
Worthington, OH 43085

Northeast Area Learning Resource Center — ME, VT
Project Director — NH, MA
384 Stockton St. — CT, RI
Highstown, NJ 08520

New York Area Learning Resource Center — NY
Project Director
New York State Education Department
Division for Handicapped Children
55 Elk St., Room 117
Albany, NY 12234

Pennsylvania Area Learning Resource Center — PA
Project Director
443 S. Gulph Rd.
King of Prussia, PA 19406

Mid-East Area Learning Resource Center	DE, DC
Project Director	NC, MD
University of Kentucky	VA, WV
Porter Building, Room 123	KY, TN
Lexington, KY 40506	

Specialized Office
Project Director
Audio-Visual Center
Indiana University
Bloomington, IN 47401

The National Center on Educational Media and
Materials for the Handicapped
NCEMMH
Project Director
Ohio Sate University
220 W. 12th Ave.
Columbus, OH 43210

Appendix C

TEACHER CERTIFICATION AGENCIES

Individuals who are interested in certification in special education can obtain information by writing to the appropriate state department of certification.

Coordinator of Teacher Education and Certification
State Department of Education
Montgomery, AL 36104

State of Alaska
Department of Education
Alaska Office Building
Pouch F.
Juneau, AK 99801

State Department of Public Instruction
Room 27, Capitol Building
Phoenix, AZ 85007

State of Arkansas
Department of Education
State Education Building
Little Rock, AR 72201

Commission for Teacher Preparation and Licensing
1020 O St., Room 222
Sacramento, CA 95814

State Department of Education
State Office Building
Denver, CO 80203

State of Connecticut
Department of Education
P.O. Box 2219
Hartford, CT 06115

State Department of Public Instruction
Dover, DE 19901

District of Columbia Public Schools
415 12th St., N.W.
Washington, DC 20004

Department of Education
Floyd T. Christian, Commissioner
Tallahassee, FL 32304

State Department of Education
Office of Instructional Services
Teacher Certification Service
State Office Building
Atlanta, GA 30334

Office of Personnel Services
State Department of Education
P.O. Box 2360
Honolulu, HI 96804

Department of Education
State of Idaho
Len B. Jordan Office Building
Boise, ID 83720

State Teacher Certification Board
212 E. Monroe St.
Springfield, IL 62706

Division of Teacher Education and Certification
Room 230 State House
Indianapolis, IN 46204

111

Department of Public Instruction
Grimes State Office Building
Des Moines, IA 50319

Kansas State Department of Education
Kansas State Education Building
120 E. 10th St.
Topeka, KS 66612

Division of Teacher Education and Certification
State Department of Education
Frankfort, KY 40601

State of Louisiana
Department of Education
P.O. Box 44064
Baton Rouge, LA 70704

Division of Professional Services
State Department of Education
Augusta, ME 04330

Maryland State Department of Education
P.O. Box 8717
BWI Airport
Baltimore, MD 21240

The Commonwealth of Massachusetts
Department of Education
182 Tremont St.
Boston, MA 02111

Michigan Department of Education
Special Education Services
Box 420
Lansing, MI 48902

State of Minnesota
Department of Education
Capitol Square
550 Cedar St.
St. Paul, MN 55101

State of Mississippi
Department of Education
P.O. Box 771
Jackson, MS 39205

State Department of Education
Division of Public Schools
P.O. Box 480
Jefferson City, MO 65101

Superintendent of Public Instruction
State Department of Public Instruction
Helena, MT 59601

State of Nebraska
Department of Education
233 S. 10th St.
Lincoln, NE 68508

Nevada Department of Education
Carson City, NV 89701

Director, Teacher Education and Professional Standards
State House Annex, Room 410
Concord, NH 03301

Department of Education
Division of Field Services
Bureau of Teacher Education and Academic Credentials
Trenton, NJ 08625

State of New Mexico
Department of Education
Education Building
Santa Fe, NM 87501

The University of the State of New York
The State Education Department
99 Washington Ave.
Albany, NY 12210

State of North Carolina
Department of Public Instruction
Raleigh, NC 27611

Department of Public Instruction
Bismarck, ND 58501

Division of Teacher Education
and Certification
1012 State Office Building
Columbus, OH 43215

State Department of Education
Oklahoma City, OK 73105

Teacher Standards and Practices
Commission
942 Lancaster Dr., Ne.
Salem, OR 97310

Commonwealth of Pennsylvania
Department of Education
Box 911
Harrisburg, PA 17126

Commonwealth of Puerto Rico
Department of Education
Hato Rey, PR 00919

State of Rhode Island and Providence Plantations
Department of Education
199 Promenade St.
Providence, RI 02908

State Department of Education
Rutledge Office Building
Columbia, SC 29201

Department of Education and
Cultural Affairs
Division of Elementary and Sec-
ondary Education
State Capitol Building
Pierre, SD 57501

Department of Education
Teacher Education and Certification
125 Cordell Hull Building
Nashville, TN 37219

Texas Education Agency
201 E. Eleventh St.
Austin, TX 78701

Utah State Board of Education
1400 University Club Building
136 E. South Temple St.
Salt Lake City, UT 86111

Vermont Department of Education
Montpelier, VT 05602

Commonwealth of Virginia
State Department of Education
Richmond, VA 23216

Superintendent of Public Instruc-
tion
Old Capitol Building
Olympia, WA 98504

State of West Virginia
State Superintendent of Schools
Department of Education
Charleston, WV 25305

State Superintendent
Department of Public Instruction
126 Langdon St.
Madison, WI 53702

Pupil Services
Casper-Midwest Schools
c/o Willard School
129 North Elk
Casper, WY 82601

Appendix D

STATE STATUTORY RESPONSIBILITIES FOR THE EDUCATION OF HANDICAPPED CHILDREN*

State	Type of Mandation	Date of Passage	Compliance Date	Ages of Eligibility	Categories Excluded
Alabama	Full Planning & Programming	1971	1977	6-12	Profoundly Retarded
Alaska	Full Program	1974		From age 3	
Arizona	Selective Planning & Programming	1973	9/76	5-21	Emotionally Handicapped
Arkansas	Full Planning & Programming[1]	1973	9/79	6-21	
California	Selective			6-18[2]	"Educationally Handicapped" (Emotionally Disturbed Learning Disabled)
Colorado	Full Planning & Programming	1973	7/75	5-21	
Connecticut	Full Planning & Programming	1966		4-21[3]	
Delaware	Full Program "Wherever Possible"			4-21	Severely Mentally or Physically Handicapped
District of Columbia	So. Statute Court Order: Full Program	1972	1972	From age 6	
Florida	Full Program		1973[4]	3-no maximum (13 yrs. guaranteed)	
Georgia	Full Planning & Programming	1968	9/75	3-20	

*The Council for Exceptional Children, 1920 Association Drive, Reston, VA 22091.

State	Type of Mandation	Date of Passage	Compliance Date	Ages of Eligibility	Categories Excluded
Hawaii	Full Program	1949		5-20	
Idaho	Full Program[5]	1972[5]		Birth-21	
Illinois	Full Program	1965	7/69	3-21[6]	
Indiana	Full Planning & Programming	1969	1973	6-18[7]	
Iowa	Full Program "If Reasonably Possible"	1974		Birth-21	
Kansas	Full Planning & Programming	1974	1979[8]	Developmentally Disabled: Birth-21	
Kentucky	Planning & Programming (Petition for Trainable Mentally Retarded only)	1970	1974	9	Other than TMR
Louisiana	Court Order-Orlenas Parish Only: Selective for Mentally Retarded Otherwise Mandatory	1962 / 1972	1972	6-21 / 3-10[10]	Other than Mentally Retarded
Maine	Full Planning & Programming	1973	1975[11]	5-20	
Maryland	Full Planning & Programming	1973	1979[12]	13	
Mass	Full Planning & Programming	1972		3-21	
Michigan	Full Planning & Programming	1971	9/73	Birth-25	
Minnesota	Full Program	7/72[14]	14	4-21, except MR (5-12) and ED (6-21)	
Mississippi	Permissive			Birth-21	
Missouri	Full Planning & Programming	1973		5-21	
Montana	Full Program[15]	1974	7/79	6-21	
Nebraska	Full Planning & Programming	1973	10/76[16]	5-18	
Nevada	Full Program	1973		5-18[17]	
N. Hampshire	Full Program			Birth-21	
New Jersey	Full Program	1954[18]		5-20	
New Mexico	Full Planning & Programming	1972	9/76	6-21[19]	
New York	Full Program	1973	1973	5-21	

State	Type of Mandation	Date of Passage	Compliance Date	Ages of Eligibility	Categories Excluded
No. Carolina	Full Planning	1974	20	Birth-Adulthood[21]	Profoundly Retarded
No. Dakota	Full Planning & Programming	1973	7/80[22]	5/21[3]	
Ohio	Permissive			Birth-21	Other than crippled or Educable Mentally Retarded, Deaf, Blind, Partial hearing or Vision
	Selective Planning	1972	1973	23	Trainable or Profoundly Mentally Retarded
Oklahoma	Full Program	1971	9/70	4-21[24]	
Oregon	Full Program	1973		EMR:6-21 / Others: Birth-21	
Pennsylvania	Court Order: Selective (Mentally Retarded Only)	1972	9/72	6-21[25]	Other than mentally retarded
Rhode Island	Full Planning & Programming	1956	1956	6-21	
So. Carolina	Full Program	1972	1964[26]	3-21[26]	
So. Dakota	Full Planning & Programming	1972	1977	6-21[27]	
Tennessee	Full Planning & Programming	1972	9/74[2]	Birth-21	
Texas	Full Program[28]	1969	9/76[28]	4-21	
Utah	Full Program	1969		3-21	
Vermont	Full Program[29]	1972		5-21	
Virginia	Full Planning	1972	30	Birth-21	
Washington	Full Program	1971		2-21	
W. Virginia	Full Program	1974	1974	6-21[31]	
Wisconsin	Full Planning & Programming	1973	8/74	5-23[32]	

State	Type of Mandation	Date of Passage	Compliance Date	Ages of Eligibility	Categories Excluded
Wyoming......Full Program		1969		6-21	

[1]Current statute is conditional: 5 or more similarly handicapped children in district. However, a 1973 Attorney General's opinion stated that the law mandating full planning and programming was effective July, 1973. If the state activates a kindergarten program for 5-year-old children, ages of eligibility will be 5-21.

[2]Permissive for children 3-21, except MR: 5 yrs. 8 mos.-21.

[3]3-21 for hearing impaired. Lower figure applies to age of child as of Jan. 1 of the school year.

[4]1973' law did not include profoundly retarded; however, a 1974 amendment brought these children under the provisions of the mandatory law. Compliance date for full services to these children is mandated for 1977-78.

[5]Earlier (1963) law was mandatory for all handicapped children except Trainable Mentally Retarded.

[6]5-21 for speech defective.

[7]Permissive 3-5 and 19-21.

[8]"Developmentally Disabled" means retardation, cerebral palsy or epilepsy. For other disabilities, the state board is to determine ages of eligibility as part of the state plan. Compliance date is 7/1/74 for DD programs.

[9]Permissive: 3-6.

[10]Residents over age 21 who were not provided educational services as children must also be given education and training opportunities.

[11]In cases of significant hardship the commissioner of education may waive enforcement until 1977.

[12]Court order sets deadline in Sept., 1975.

[13]Services must begin as soon as the child can benefit from them, whether or not he is of school age.

[14]Date on which Trainable Mentally Retarded were included under the previously existing mandatory law.

[15]Statute now in effect is selective and conditional: at least 10 Educable Mentally Retarded, 7 Trainable Mentally Retarded, or 10 physically handicapped in school district. Full mandation becomes effective 7/1/79.

[16]Acoustically handicapped: 10/1/74.

[17]Aurally handicapped and visually handicapped: birth-18.

[18]Date of original mandatory law, which has since been amended to include all children.

Appendix E

KEY MEMBERS OF U.S. CONGRESS

95th CONGRESS

Members of the Committees of the U.S. Congress having jurisdiction over most authorizing legislation at the Federal level affecting the education of exceptional children.

SENATE COMMITTEE ON HUMAN RESOURCES

Jurisdiction: Education and Labor Legislation

Room	Democrats	Telephone
352	Harrison Williams, Jr., NJ, Chairman	224-4744
5121	Jennings Randolph, WV	224-6472
325	Claiborne Pell, RI	224-4642
431	Edward Kennedy, MA	224-4543
221	Gaylord Nelson, WI	224-5323
6235	Thomas Eagleton, MO	224-5721
452	Alan Cranston, CA	224-3553
248	William Hathaway, ME	224-2523
253	Don Riegle, MI	224-4822
	Republicans	
321	Jacob Javits, NY, Ranking Minority Member	224-6542
347	Richard Schweiker, PA	224-4254
5219	Robert Stafford, VT	224-5141
115A	Orrin Hatch, UT	224-5251
3125	John Chafee, RI	224-2921
6221	S.I. Hayakawa, CA	224-3841

Majority Staff: Lisa Walker 224-9161 6302 Dirksen
Minority Staff: Jay Cutler 224-2705 4222 Dirksen

HANDICAPPED SUBCOMMITTEE OF THE
HUMAN RESOURCES COMMITTEE

Jurisdiction: Handicapped Legislation, Including Education

Room	Democrats	Telephone
5121	Jennings Randolph, WV, Chairman	224-6472
352	Harrison Williams, NJ	224-4744
6235	Thomas Eagleton, MO	224-5721

Majority Staff: Patricia Forsythe 224-9075 4230 Dirksen

Room	Republicans	Telephone
5219	Robert Stafford, VT Ranking Minority Member	224-5141
115A	Orrin Hatch, UT	224-5251

Minority Staff: Jackson Andrews 224-7682 4230 Dirksen

EDUCATION, ARTS AND HUMANITIES SUBCOMMITTEE
OF THE HUMAN RESOURCES COMMITTEE

Jurisdiction: Education, Including Education of
Gifted and Talented Children

Room	Democrats	Telephone
325	Claiborne Pell, RI, Chairman	224-4642
5121	Jennings Randolph, WV	224-6472
431	Edward Kennedy, MA	224-4543
6235	Thomas Eagleton, MO	224-5721

Majority Staff: Jean Frohlicher 224-7666 4228 Dirksen

Room	Republicans	Telephone
5219	Robert Stafford, VT, Ranking Minority Member	224-5141
347	Richard Schweiker, PA	224-4245
6221	S.I. Hayakawa, CA	224-3841
321	Jacob Javits, NY, ex officio	224-6542

Minority Staff: Gregory Fusco 224-7688 4222 Dirksen

HOUSE COMMITTEE ON EDUCATION AND LABOR

Jurisdiction: Education and Labor Legislation in General

Room	Democrats	Telephone
2365	Carl Perkins, KY, Chairman	225-4935
2109	Frank Thompson, Jr., NJ	225-3765
2104	John Dent, PA	225-5631
1236	John Brademas, IN	225-3915
2350	Augustus Hawkins, CA	225-2201
2368	William Ford, MI	225-6261
2454	Phillip Burton, CA	225-4965
2238	Joseph Gaydos, PA	225-4631
2264	William Clay, MO	225-2406
2421	Mario Biaggi, NY	225-2464
228	Ike Andrews, NC	225-1784
213	Michael Blouin, IA	225-2911
1512	Robert Cornell, WI	225-5665
227	Paul Simon, IL	225-5201
131	Edward Beard, RI	225-2735
215	Leo Zeferetti, NY	225-4105
1531	George Miller, CA	225-2095
1233	Ronald Mottl, OH	225-5731
1331	Michael Myers, PA	225-4731
1118	Austin Murphy, PA	225-4665
507	Joseph LeFante, NY	225-2765
1229	Ted Weiss, NY	225-5635
322	Cecil Heftel, HI	225-2726
1319	Baltasar Corrada, PR	225-2615
503	Dale Kildee, MI	225-3611

Room	Republicans	Telephone
2185	Albert Quie, MN, Ranking Minority Member	225-2271
1436	John Ashbrook, OH	225-6431
2236	John Erienborn, IL	225-3515
229	Ronald Sarasin, CT	225-3822
2159	John Buchanan, AL	225-4921
429	James Jeffords, VT	225-4115

Room	Republicans	Telephone
1132	Larry Pressler, SD	225-2801
1713	William Goodling, PA	225-5836
1112	Bud Shuster, PA	225-2431
1421	Shirley Pettis, CA	225-5861
1709	Carl Pursell, MI	225-4401
1223	Mickey Edwards, OK	225-2132

Majority Staff: 225-4527 2181 Rayburn

Jack Reed-Elementary, Secondary, vocational education
Bill Gaul-Postsecondary education, select programs
    and higher education

Minority Staff 225-4527 2179 Rayburn

Christopher Cross-ESEA, NIE, guaranteed student loans
Charles Radcliffe-Vocational education, school lunch
Martin LaVor-Child development, Handicapped
Robert Andrings-Higher education

SELECT EDUCATION SUBCOMMITTEE OF THE EDUCATION AND LABOR COMMITTEE

Jurisdiction: Select Education Programs, Handicapped Education, Arts and Humanities

Room	Democrats	Telephone
1236	John Brademas, IN, Chairman	225-3915
131	Edward Beard, RI	225-2735
1531	George Miller, CA	225-2095
503	Dale Kildee, MI	225-3611
322	Cecil Heftel, HI	225-2726
2350	Augustus Hawkins, CA	225-2201
2421	Mario Biaggi, NY	225-2464

Room	Republicans	Telephone
429	James Jeffords, VT, Ranking Minority Member	225-4115
1132	Larry Pressler, SD	225-2801

Majority Staff: Jack Duncan 225-5954   2178 Rayburn
Minority Staff: See Education and Labor Committee Minority Staff

BUILDING ADDRESS CODE

House

Three-digit room number: Cannon House Office Building
Four-digit room number (where the first digit is 1): Longworth House Office Building
Four-digit room number (where the first digit is 2): Rayburn House Office Building
  Zip code for House: 20515

Senate

Three-digit room number: Russell Senate Office Building
Four-digit room number: Dirksen Senate Office Building
  Zip code for Senate: 20510

Telephone Area Code: 202

NAME INDEX

SUBJECT INDEX

A

Administration, 23-26
federal, 24
local, 27, 28, 41-45
state, 26, 27, 30, 39, 40
Advocacy groups, 103-105
citizen, 12, 43, 44, 70, 85
professional, 45
Alpen-Boll Developmental Profile, 53
American Federation of Teachers, 29, 59
American National Standards Institute,
98
American Printing House for the Blind, 3
Assessment tests, 26, 62
Association for Children With Learning
Disabilities, 45, 103

B

Barrier-free architecture, 97, 98
compliance, vii
funding, 22, 23
Bilingual education, 14
Board of Cooperative Educational Service
(BOCES), 40
Brain injured, 83, *see also* Learning dis-
abilities
Bureau of Education for the Handicapped
(BEH), 30, 31, 54, 81, 83, 84, 88-93

C

Civil Rights Act, 14, 99
Classroom organization, 72-78
physical education, 27
resource rooms, 49
segregated, v, 47
Comprehensive Test of Basic Skills, 77
Council of Administrators of Special Education (CASE), 88, 95

Council for Exceptional Children (CEC),
xi, 11, 25, 45, 69
Curriculum, 46-49, 88

D

Disabilities
blind, 94
deaf, 93, 94
definitions, 19, 20
learning disabilities, 79-88
severely impaired, 40
Down's syndrome, 54, 55
Due process, 28-31
arbitration, 12
objections, 29, 30
rights of parents, 29
State of Michigan, 12
Dyslexia, 82, *see also* Learning disabilities

E

Early childhood education, 50-55
Eastern Michigan University, xi
Educational Facilities Laboratory (EFL),
98
Education For All Handicapped Children
Act, ix, 17-32
annual authorization, 7
co-mingled funds, 26
confusion, xiii
congressional findings, xiii, 18
cooperative district funding, 25
curtailment of federal monies, 28, 30
excess costs, 22
funding for, 17, 23-25, 93, 98
financial reporting, 30
legislative hearings, xiii
passed by congress, xiii
public policy, 9
requirements, ix

125

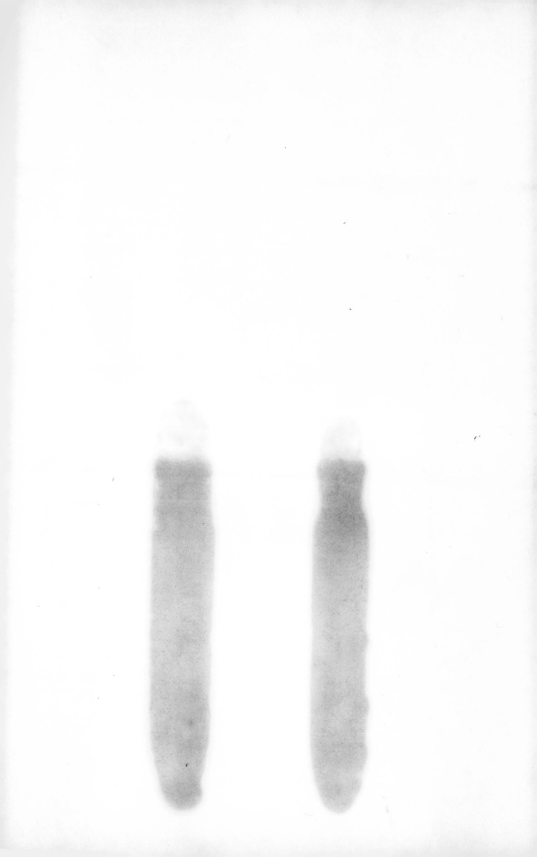